THE TEACHING CHURCH— ACTIVE IN MISSION

PAUL D. AND
KATHERINE A. GEHRIS

Judson Press ® Valley Forge

*This book is dedicated to **Jitsuo Morikawa**, who, when the authors were very young in the pastoral ministry, helped us to see the inextricable relationship betweeen evangelism and mission, and to **Lois and J. Richard Hawley**, who showed us directly at the congregational level how mission and evangelism can happen together.*

THE TEACHING CHURCH—ACTIVE IN MISSION

Copyright © 1987
Judson Press, Valley Forge, PA 19482-0851

Unless otherwise indicated, Scripture quotations in this volume are from the Revised Standard Version of the Bible, copyrighted 1946, 1952, © 1971, 1973 by the Division of Christian Education of the National Council of the Churches of Christ in the U.S.A., and used by permission.

Library of Congress Cataloging-in-Publication Data

Gehris, Katherine A.
   The teaching church active in mission.

   1. Mission of the church.   I. Gehris, Paul D.
II. Title.
BV601.8.G35   1987   266   87-3696
ISBN 0-8170-1080-7

Contents

Foreword

The Teaching Church–Active in Mission

For many people involved in the tasks of Christian education, it has been helpful in recent years to think in terms of the five *functions* of a teaching church. The functions have been described as

- *affirming* the foundations of the teaching ministry,
- *planning* for an effective teaching ministry,
- *developing leaders* for a variety of ministries,
- *nurturing* persons in Christian growth,
- *enabling* the church's mission in the world.

It is the intention of Katherine and Paul Gehris, through the content of *The Teaching Church—Active in Mission*, to help us with the concept of *enabling the church's mission in the world*. This is the third book in a series of resources for the teaching church.[1]

It is possible that in times past we have conceived of the experiences contained in the Christian education framework as ends within themselves. The Gehrises believe in the educational ministry of the church, and it is their strong desire that the outcome of education will be involvement in mission.

To bring this about, they introduce us to a term. It is the word "missioner." The word describes persons "who are actively engaged in mission, beginning where they are and continuing to the 'farthest corners of creation.'" It is their intention that the teaching ministry of the church call per-

[1] The first book in the teaching church series was *Developing Leadership in the Teaching Church* by Jan Chartier. The second was *Foundations for the Teaching Church* by Grant W. Hanson. Both were published by Judson Press.

sons to be missioners.

Their efforts in the text are practical and exciting. They provide us with a foundation in which we understand that the whole church is called to do the mission of God. They help us look at ways in which the educational ministry of the church can call and prepare missioners. They offer opportunity for us to see that all of God's people can be missioners. Finally, they provide direction, suggestions, and support for the development of missioners in each church.

Paul and Katherine Gehris are missioners in their own lives! Through this book they invite all to join them in doing God's work.

John L. Carroll

Director

Division of Church Education
American Baptist Churches
Valley Forge, Pennsylvania

Introduction

The teaching church has many responsibilities related to teaching and learning. It is the goal of this short book to clarify what some of those responsibilities are in the area of mission and to offer some tools to our teachers so that our churches can be more active in mission.

Some of the ideas shared in this book may be "old hat" to some; other ideas my be refreshingly new. All of the ideas have potential if they are rightly understood and implemented.

We need "missioners"—members of our churches who are actively engaged in mission—doing mission intentionally, based on our understanding of the gospel and the needs of our world. This world begins where we are and continues to the farthest corners of creation.

Chapter 1 will strongly make the point that the whole church is called to do the mission of God—sharing the Good News of creation and life made new through Jesus Christ. Persons who do this sharing are called missioners.

Chapter 2 looks at the educational process and the ways churches can educate people to be missioners. It makes suggestions for each stage of human development.

Chapter 3 looks at vocation and avocation. It challenges us as churches to lead the way for people to be missioners at work and at play.

Chapter 4 looks at evangelism and mission; it speaks to the needs of both and helps us to see ways to implement each in our church life and outreach.

Chapter 5 speaks to unity of purpose and action among churches—denominationally and ecumenically. It suggests ways your church could join with others to strengthen the impact of your mission.

Chapter 6 gives planning aids and suggestions. Its contention is that planning unifies efforts and vision and enables mission.

The study guide suggests ways to use this book and enable your congregation to explore its mission. It also provides questions that members, boards, and committees can ask themselves as they clarify their roles as missioners.

1
The Role of the Church in the Mission of God

Vignette: There is an old apocryphal story about Jesus and the disciples being in conversation after the resurrection. It has become clear that Jesus' time with the eleven was limited, and, in light of his ministry, there was some anxiety about the future without him. Those who heard the Good News gladly and those who needed to hear it were a matter of concern. The small minority of the Pharisees and their sort who had hounded him, even to his death, was a matter of concern as well. What was to happen now? What was to happen next? Jesus told the disciples that the Spirit would come to them and empower them and that everything would work out for them. "But," they asked, "what if it doesn't work out for us? Don't you have another plan? You must have something else in mind if it doesn't work!" Jesus' response was emphatic. "You are the plan! There is no other plan!" And so there was not because there did not need to be. They were the plan. WE ARE THE PLAN. THE CHURCH IS THE PLAN.

The Church in Historical Context

It is the purpose of this chapter to see the church as part of an old and wonderful historical tradition from Abraham to the present. We will also describe the people of God, the church, as an inclusive people who both hear and "do" the Good News of the gospel as "missioners." Part of our work together will be discussed. The chapter closes with a list of characteristics of missioners who ARE THE PLAN.

The church is the latest and the last breakthrough in God's dealing with creation. In our recorded religious history, as humanity has been ready, God has dealt with people. (It is important to note here that the authors are quite aware that different schools of thought assign various timetables to the periods that date back to an original creation event. With due respect to all the theories, the authors assume the historical reality of Abraham living about 4000 B.C. Thus God's work with those of us on this planet began about six thousand years ago, a mere quick click in terms of time, but the most important time in terms of the maturation of humanity.

In God's time a message went to a man named Abram that there was a better way. Abram became Abraham. The better way was to affirm "one God" and go to the place of promise to which the "one God" would lead. The promise also included that the progeny of Abraham would be as numerous as the stars of the sky and the sands of the sea. The promise was in the process of fulfillment during the lives of Isaac and Jacob and Joseph. A major breakthrough occurred when Moses, after hundreds of years of captivity for God's people, demanded in the name of God that the people be set free. They were. Not handling freedom well, they vacillated in their devotion to the One who had freed them. Judges were raised up by God—both male and female judges—to bring help and hope to the people. There were the prophets, priests, and kings, and around 1000 B.C. the highest point of the Jewish nation was reached under King David. After David's reign the Jewish nation declined, with outside forces sometimes bringing the Jews under subjugation. Even the intercession of prophets could not prevent this subjugation. It is interesting to note that when the people were free from outside oppression, they were known to oppress their own people, usually the poor and the powerless. From about the year 400 to the changing of the eras (B.C. to A.D.) there was silence—no word from the Lord. Then came John the Baptist announcing Jesus and Jesus announcing the kingdom of God and the disciples and the church, which was created and empowered by the Holy

Spirit. The church, which is now about two thousand years old (a very brief historical resume is given in chapter 5), is empowered by the same Spirit to do the same mission as the earliest apostles. We are to announce the Good News of the gospel, that Christ has redeemed the world and that life can be different. Those who are announcers are modern day "missioners."

The Church Described

The church is made up of the people of God who know they are God's people. The church is the called out/responding people of God. The church is well described, if not defined, by Peter in his first letter: "You are a chosen race, a royal priesthood, a holy nation, God's own people, that you may declare the wonderful deeds of him who called you out of darkness into his marvelous light. Once you were no people but now you are God's people; once you had not received mercy but now you have received mercy" (1 Peter 2:9-10). This church of which Peter speaks is an inclusive church. Paul states it clearly: "There is neither Jew nor Greek, there is neither slave nor free, there is neither male nor female; for you are all one in Christ Jesus. And if you are Christ's, then you are Abraham's offspring, heirs according to promise" (Galatians 3:28-29). Today we could add "neither white nor color, neither old nor young, neither rich nor poor, neither eastern nor western, neither northern nor southern, neither upper nor middle nor lower class." The church is the whole people of God even though we have created many divisions. The divisions suit our hardened hearts, clouded minds, and grasping reach for earthly power. We have among us all the parts and share all the gifts and are the recipients of the same grace. The church most of us know best is our "hands on" part of the church called the congregation. In the early years of its history the church was a municipally oriented structure— Galatia, Rome, Ephesus, Laodicea, Philadelphia, and so forth. There was a group of believers, the church, in a city.

Ultimately the church became denominational and congregational, not municipal. Despite the divisions, however, each part is a piece of the whole. The writer once served a congregation in a small town in northeastern Pennsylvania. There was one other mainline congregation in the town. It was, and is, a two-church town. When it was decided to put welcome signs at the town limits along the major highway, we resisted saying "The Baptist Church and the Methodist Church Welcome You." After considerable discussion the sign said

---

The Church at Factoryville Welcomes You

Baptist	Methodist
Worship 11 A.M.	Worship 11 A.M.
Church School 9:45 A.M.	Church School 9:45 A.M.

---

indicating the one church with two denominations and congregations.

The role of the church is to make the announcement of the Good News, to model in its structure and through its people the Good News and the implications of the Good News, and to challenge itself and the world to hear and heed the message. This is a modern paradigm of what Jesus did himself at his home synagogue in Nazareth.

> . . . and he went to the synagogue, as his custom was, on the sabbath day. And he stood up to read; and there was given to him the book of the prophet Isaiah. He opened the book and found the place where it was written,
> "The Spirit of the Lord is upon me,
> because he has anointed me to preach good news to the poor.
> He has sent me to proclaim release to the captives
> and recovering of sight to the blind,
> to set at liberty those who are oppressed,
> to proclaim the acceptable year of the Lord."
> —Luke 4:16-19

This was the announcement; he modeled it in his ministry and challenged the world to heed it. The big difference between us and Jesus is the matter of faithfulness and obedience to God. We fall short. Realizing that we are not sinless junior Jesuses but sinners who know Jesus Christ, we can take some of the pressure off ourselves. Mission for us is not what Jesus would do but what Jesus would have us do.

The Church and Culture

Whether we like it or not, the church is part of a cultural milieu that needs to be considered by missioners. Mission should include Good News to the spirit, mind, and body without having to worry unduly about cultural idiosyncrasies. Such things as clothing styles, educational attainment, power and prestige, station in life, and economic and political beliefs may have meaning to individuals. The Good News, however, is not changed by these things. Ultimately, these cultural parts of life may be changed by the Good News.

To be part of a cultural milieu but not captured by the alien values of the culture is almost impossible, but we must nevertheless do our best to be unconquered by our culture. It is important to clarify mission values without an overlay of cultural values. The gospel dare not be domesticated to cultural norms and/or expectations. We need to be aware of the cult of materialism in America that easily can prostitute our understanding of the gospel. Fortunately, after Jesus said that it is easier for a camel to go through the eye of a needle than for a rich man to enter the kingdom of God, he added that with God all things are possible. Middle-class Americans are in the top one percent of the richest people in known history, yet middle-class congregations tend to spend more on their church buildings than on mission. These Christians have forgotten that the good life in America and the new life in Christ are not necessarily the same. Indeed, the good life in America could keep people from seeking the kingdom of God, believing that they have already found it in their comfortable life here. We also get caught by the overimportance of our religious institution, or theology, or creeds, both written and unwritten, and even our personal and cultural ideas about styles of life.

Just as the church needs to be aware of cultural differences, we need to be aware that our denomination and our congregation often reflect our culture. It's neither good nor bad, right nor wrong; it simply is. Rather than deny or deify the cultural trappings of the church we know, we can ignore what is not helpful and use whatever is helpful for our mission. The church is not without wrinkle, spot, or blemish as we someday will be. The church on earth is a reflection of those comprising it. Our claim is faith, not perfection. What makes the church unique is that while it is a human institution, flawed and imperfect, it is also a manifestation of God's love and compassion and has been given the responsibility for mission. Humans did not form the church; they merely formalized it. The church was created by the power of God and as such is unique as an institution in our society. The uniqueness is not seen in special privilege but in willingness to serve—to be involved in mission.

The Mission of the Church

The mission of the church is multifaceted. In Jesus' mission statement, taken from Isaiah, we are confronted and comforted by Good News for the whole creation. We carry that forward. There is concern for body, mind, and soul. There is need for sharing bread for the belly and the "bread of life." For the church to be involved in mission we must be able to see and comprehend the world in which we live, from our neighborhood and parish to the outermost ends of the earth. This does not mean knowing all the facts and figures; it does mean knowing something of the needs, the people, the problems. The old divisions for mission are obliterated. We see the whole world as an interdependent piece. Once there were foreign missions; the word "foreign" was changed to "overseas" and finally to "international." That part of mission was juxtaposed against home missions, which meant places in our country that were not always or even usually near us. Even for mainline congregations neighborhood mission often meant another neighborhood. Not so any longer. All mission is part of the whole—from myself and my household to the edge of known habitation. Concern for debris in space is an ecological mission going beyond where any person exists—at least at the present time.

In some churches nonsmokers and nondrinkers are considered to be on the higher spiritual level than smokers and drinkers. The church has a temperance standard. We know that abuse of alcohol and abuse of tobacco is unhealthy (so is overeating), but abstinence (or at least moderation) is not a part of the entrance requirements for the kingdom. We have a tendency to create our own dogma—the amount of water used for baptism, the absence of a written creed, and biblical interpretation of which we are absolutely, unequivocally certain. Jesus criticized the cocksure religious leaders when he said they laid heavy burdens on the people and did not help to lift them. The task of mission is not to weigh down but to "free up"—to liberate—apart from culture, money, theology, or practice.

Reconciliation and Healing

Mission includes reconciliation and healing. We live in a world of five billion souls (on July 7, 1986, probably in a Third World country, the five billionth inhabitant of the planet Earth was born, according to the World Population Institute). At least one billion will live at the edge of indescribable poverty and ill health and will die early. At the national level that same statistic prevails; 20 percent of Americans live at the edge or over the edge of poverty with all its accompanying problems. One of the tasks of mission is to decide how seriously to take any kind of responsibility to these people, be they in the neighborhood, city, state, country, or world. The Old Testament call to justice and mercy and the New Testament call to love force us to take these people seriously. People who have physical or mental disabilities, those who are poverty-stricken, sick, homeless, helpless, jobless—these people have first claim on the Good News. Jesus said that the well have no need of a physician, but the sick and the down-and-out need to be sought out. The mission of which we speak is multifaceted. It meets people where they are. It feeds, clothes, shelters, and protects them. It educates, finds jobs, and enriches their lives. It embodies the Good News of the gospel and speaks the Good News in deeds and words. It strives to bring wholeness and relationship and self-respect. Mission meets people where they are and goes with them where they need to go.

Missioners at Work

As has been indicated, the doers of mission are missioners. We have missionaries who go far and wide. Other missionaries stay near home. The concept of mission needs missionaries who are specially called and set aside to do mission. Along with these folks, *all* those who have heard and taken seriously the Good News are missioners. Our churches should be filled with them. Some of God's work in mission may even be done by those who neither know, accept, or understand God. Because they do good for others, they satisfy the teaching of Jesus that whoever is not against us is for us. It is not for us to be jealous or haughty when others do good for God's creation but not in God's name. We can rejoice that the mysterious and inscrutable Spirit of God works in wondrous ways.

Most missioners, however, are church folk. They take the gospel seriously. They rejoice in what God has done and is doing for them and so want to share Good News. Not all church people are ready to do mission. If they are part of the church for cultural or business reasons, if they are caught up in the need for an ever-rising standard of living, if they are driven by a frenetic lifestyle so that the church helps them breathe, then we must wait for them. Indeed they need to be receivers of mission—to catch up to the meaning of spiritual rebirth, which helps people realize that their lives have been cluttered with more wants than needs.

For those who are ready to be involved in mission there is no dearth of opportunity. There is something for everyone. It is important for the institutional church to offer a wide spectrum of mission programs so that people are neither overwhelmed nor left unchallenged. Some folks respond to a call to mission that is simple. Other folks might be put off by anything other than a very difficult task. Without being classist or elitist, the writer believes that some of the best and brightest persons in the church have not been challenged by the church to get involved in mission because we have asked so little. God honors all who do mission. We honor persons by challenging them to the limit of their ability. Mission is impossible apart from the laity. Although clergy and other professionals in the church do mission as their vocation, it is the laity, which comprises over 99 percent of the church, that gets mission done. We fool one another and miss the apostle Paul's point about the gifts in the church if we place one person higher than the other. Clergy and professionals and laity have significance roles to play. They play them best when they are seen as part of the whole body of the church.

Discipline

In order to be effective, missioners need to be intentional and focused—disciplined. In some circles today discipline is understood to be negative. Discipline comes from the word "disciple." Discipline means accomplishing our goals by accepting challenges. Sometimes we try to avoid discipline; it may be inconvenient or even disagreeable. The vignette of Jesus in prayer in the Gethsemane garden tells us a lot about discipline. He prayed so fervently that his sweat was like drops of blood. His prayer asked for the possible avoidance of the challenge of the cross. Discipline helped him to accept the challenge. We also have challenges to accept, and discipline will see us through.

The mission of the church is best accomplished when personal involvement and institutional goals are integrated. For instance, when local congregations are involved in setting the mission goals of their denomination, they feel an ownership of these goals and participate willingly in working toward their implementation. When church members see themselves as part of a team rather than "loners," the church's mission will be successful. To this end the concept of "independence" is not biblical. The mission of the church, like the church itself, is interdependent. The implications are clear for denominations, churches, and church agencies. They need to be open and inclusive and model interdependence. When individuals see themselves as part of the whole church, they are in a position to be fed on the prayer energy raised up for the whole church. Indeed, the thought is breathtaking—each Christian not only part of the great cloud of witnesses gone before but also part of about one billion souls in today's world who name the name of Christ.

Characteristics of Missioners

In the early history of the church the people who took Jesus seriously were called "followers of the way." They were known for loving one another and being fearless in whatever their belief brought them or cost them. They were the first missioners. Some of the characteristics of missioners today include:

Commitment. They have heard and seen the glory of the Lord in their own lives.

Seeing visions and dreaming dreams. They can look at the world that is and see something better in its place. They do not feel "stuck" with what is but "smitten" with what could be.

Movement towards wholeness. These people are in the process of becoming the best that they can be. As they are enabled by the Spirit of God, they are open to growth of character. They are not stuck with themselves even though they appreciate themselves as they are.

Realism. Their visions and dreams do not prevent a hard-nosed realism about the world as it is. They live with their heads in the air, their feet on the ground, and their hands involved in the real world.

A sense of love and justice. The injustices in society and the cruelty that is rampant are recognized, but with the recognition comes a desire to make changes. Missioners seek a world that has peace with justice, a world healed completely from the inside, not patched from the outside.

Respect for others. People who are different neither frighten nor anger the missioners. They are respected as brothers and sisters in the image of God. The aim of mission is not to make them like the missioners but to present them with opportunities as unique creatures of God.

A sense of humor. Missioners can laugh at themselves and the foibles of their own personalities. They can also laugh at the perpetrators of malice and injustice—not because they are funny but because they are ultimately losers. They can laugh at our institutions—not because they cannot produce some good but because we give them absurd powers (by our standards) and wonder why they can be so dysfunctional.

Ability to live with tension. Missioners realize that there are no final answers to our own quest or the quest of the missions of the church. In many of us there is a great need to know the ending. (Some people even read the end of the book before starting at the beginning.) While there is the biblical promise that everything will work out in the long run, it would be comforting to know the outcome. To this extent mission is a leap of faith. We are told that if we leap to God by faith, we will be caught, but we cannot experience the catching unless we take the leap. Missioners show a willingness to work and leave the results to God.

Enjoyment of the faith of the Spirit. Missioners enjoy love, joy, peace, patience, kindness, goodness, faithfulness, gentleness, and self-control. Missioners are not only serving God and the creation; they are also filling their own lives with good things, such as the fruit of the Spirit, because they are coming to be at one with the Spirit as they are led by the Spirit.

2
Education for Mission

This chapter is directed at education for mission. It attempts to define education, to outline some educational tasks, and to explore ways that mission could be incorporated into the educational planning process.

What is Education for Mission?

The dictionary says to educate is to develop the facilities and powers of by teaching, instructing or schooling; to quality by instruction or training for a particular calling or practice. Some people think that one is educated when one knows a lot of facts about a specific subject; others think that facts are less important than the ability to find the answers to the questions that arise in a given area; and still others think that the educated person is one who learns from the past in order to plan for the future. All are right but not exclusive. Education is a continuous process of seeking, discovering, and assimilating. It is a movement from unknowing to knowing. We've all experienced the motivation to find the answer to some question. We read a book or ask an authority, and we find some answers; but we also find more questions. We know more and become aware that we know less. So we ask the new questions and find out more answers. We might even become experts on certain subjects, all the time discovering that there is even more to know.

When we are open to the unfolding of knowledge, God's continuous revelation to us, we are at the same time teachers and learners. We become both missioners and the recipients of the mission.

Education is not just knowing; it is also doing. We know because someone else said so and/or we know because we tried it out and it worked, or it only worked if we did it a certain way. Some of us know a lot about things that we have never experienced; others of us have had much experience but little documentation of what we know. We need to integrate our knowledge with our actions in order to live lives that speak with authority. That is what education for mission is all about—speaking, acting, and living lives that tell of God's love. Mission is a way of life, and education is a missionary effort. It is an attitude as well as a structure. When a church knows, speaks, acts, and focuses upon its mission, the church is living that mission. Education for mission needs to combine the knowledge of the Scriptures with usable skills, self-confidence, awareness of environmental needs and resources (local and global), and a supportive community. It is not always enough to tell people "Go and preach the Word." Mission must first respond to the needs of the church members who in turn respond to the needs of people outside the church. The ripple effect can be felt around the world.

When this author spoke to friends about writing a book on enabling mission, each had a comment. A nurse/social worker said, "Tell people to begin in their own communities." A farmer said, "I can only affect the world I see and the people I talk to. I try to make responsible use of the land and resources. That in itself is a lot." The teacher and facilitator of a parents' support group said, "People need to learn how to be parents. That's a tough, challenging, and often thankless job, and many parents have no idea what is involved. Teaching effective parenting skills can change the world." A mother whose seventeen-year-old son committed suicide said, "We need to listen to one another more. There are so many clues we miss." Education for mission is more than talking to missionaries, it's being aware of the world in which we live and responding to its needs with our gifts and resources.

Education–A Continuous Process

The mission educational goal of the church is to instill in each person a sense of history, unity, and vision. (In ways that each age level can comprehend, there needs to be an understanding of the local, national, and world mission involvement of the church and the denomination.) There need to be opportunities for firsthand contact with representatives from different cultures in the community, the nation, and the world. Contact with experienced missioners helps to stimulate learners to try their own efforts at being missioners. There need to be opportunities for people of all ages and at all stages of development to give support to the mission concerns of their local church and of their denomination. People need to be able to explore and act in relation to such issues as world hunger, the use of nuclear weapons, the social and economic forces shaping families, women's rights, concerns of people who are physically or mentally disabled, and so forth. The attitude "We've always been a mission people" grows out of a personal sense of connection to the history of the church and the denomination. The attitude "We're in this together; let's work it out" grows out of a knowledge of oneself and a sense of belonging to the body of Christ. With the historical perspective and the community bonding, people can begin to envision changes. The attitude becomes "What can we do? How will it best be carried out? Come on! Let's go for it!"

Let's assume that as a church we have agreed upon a mission—to communicate God's message of love to the world. We see it as our sole purpose for being, our direct call, our faith responses to God's love for us. We have named and claimed our purpose. We recognize that this is an enormous task. There is much to do, and we begin to plan. We become aware of the fact that even as we are planning how we can best carry out our mission, we are in the process of doing it. We are learning about the difficulties and blessings of loving ourselves and one another, of trusting God's love in situations of stress, disagreement, and nitty-gritty everyday tasks. Our mission has started before we have even begun to plan how to carry it out. We also notice that the very thing we are commissioned to teach is a lesson that we are struggling to learn. How can we tell the world about God's love when we don't fully comprehend this love ourselves?

Even as we recognize that we are in the middle of something that has no beginning and no end (God's love is like that), let's attempt to make some order out of the educational process. So how do we educate for mission?

Think about how people learn. Our call as educators is to help people to know God's love for all creation by

- telling the story of the gospel,
- telling how others have responded,
- inviting people to tell their faith stories,
- relating our stories to God's promises,
- helping people to reflect upon and learn from their experiences,
- supporting and challenging people to try again in response to new awareness.

Telling the Story of the Gospel

People of all ages need to know that God loves them. Because we are individuals, we have different learning styles and different attitudes and life experiences. All these affect our ability to hear the message "God loves you . . . more than you can comprehend. God's love is never failing." Our task as educators is to tell and retell the stories in ways that they can be heard. Consider the fact that some people take in information visually (pictures, the printed word, charts, maps, videos, graphs). Others comprehend better by hearing (tape, reading aloud, storytelling, song). Some people are more receptive to learning kinesthetically (touch, drama, puppets, dance, movement). People of all ages learn through their own awareness and understanding.

Young children need to hear the story in ways that they can integrate. Most people learn by repetition. Hearing the story in different settings, at different times, with fresh perspectives is helpful. Hearing how others have responded to the love of God is another way of telling the story.

Being told about the love of God while in a loving atmosphere helps people to integrate here and now feelings with the knowledge. The opportunity to tell the story yourself is a way of rehearing it. When we prepare to tell others, we tend to be intentional about the information we take in.

The Educational Task and Challenge

The educational task and challenge is to communicate the love of God through our attitude, our words, and our actions. As Christian educators, we encourage other people to reach out to God as we reach out to them. We look for ways to support, encourage, and teach in each relationship, whether it is with individuals or with a class/group. People learn by doing, so the church should provide opportunities for people to participate in mission locally and nationally. Invite people from different cultures and countries to tell their stories to your learners. In other words, find ways to expand their thinking, questioning, and exploring. Expose them and yourself to different people, places, and perspectives.

An example of encouragement at an early age is the whole issue of giving and receiving with the very young. When a baby spontaneously offers a spoonful of his or her food and it is accepted with thanks and appreciation, he or she is more apt to offer again. Too often we refuse the natural sharing of a gooey kiss or a taste of pablum (ugh!) and later wonder why it is difficult to teach toddlers to share. We as educators are not to judge the response or the timing of the response to God's call but to lay the groundwork for the process.

Invite people to tell their faith stories. The educational process is one of hearing, responding, telling. As we tell our stories, the story of the gospel comes alive. As we tell our stories to one another, we relive the experience; we enrich our collective experience; and we gain support. In listening to someone tell his or her story, we communicate respect and interest. We learn more about the person and God's revelation through that person. We model the gospel message as we try to teach it. Sharing our experiences gives us an opportunity to recognize likenesses and differences and to value them.

Provide opportunities for people to reflect upon and learn from their experience. Experience itself is a strong teacher, but when we take time to reflect upon our experiences and relate them to the call to mission, we generalize learnings that will enrich our ministry and future experience. People need time to do this reflection individually (praying, writing in a journal, seeking a quiet retreat) and collectively (listening, asking questions, pointing out similarities and biblical truths, giving feedback and suggestions, offering insights and support).

Educators need support and challenge. It's easy to become discouraged, to expect too much of ourselves and the church, to take on more than we can accomplish. Some of us take on large global tasks when it is even a challenge to interact and communicate with a co-worker, parent, or child.

Education for mission requires a stated purpose, an educational plan, clear communication of that plan to all members, commitment of as many members as possible, a supportive network, resources, implementation of the plan, evaluation, and ongoing enrichment and renewal. The process is cyclical—it is an action and a reflection process.

We do it.
We talk about it.
We evaluate it.
We pray about it.
We plan it.

We organize for action.
We do better this time.
We gather resources.
We listen to those we educate.
We learn better ways.
We try again.

Education is both planned and unplanned. We plan activities and experiences that help teach a concept. At the same time life presents experiences all the time. We can incorporate these life situations into our educational program if we are alert. At every level of our formal program we talk about and model an action-oriented response to the gospel. The church which assumes that a mission emphasis is intentional tends to foster that way of life in its members.

What Does It Mean to Be Intentional About Education for Mission?

Although everyone concerned with Christian education should be mission oriented, the mission emphasis can get lost. It is helpful to assign one member of the board of education to focus on mission. That person's responsibility is to keep mission alive, to be aware of what other churches and denominations are doing, to explore local, national, and international needs, to report these needs to the board, to suggest ways to integrate mission into the curriculum and the program, to tell mission stories, and to invite others to tell mission stories. The mission education person (or committee) also gives input to the budget and helps decide upon and enrich curriculum. The mission education person contributes to whatever decisions are made by the church educational body.

Even when a church integrates the mission emphasis into its total educational programs, it is worthwhile to have a school of mission or a day of mission occasionally. This is a time for a special focus on outreach. It could be the study of the political process and how to effectively bring about change. It could be an exchange trip to or from another country or a work camp or a series of workshops on ecological needs. It might be a skills training event on communication, conflict management, negotiation, family systems, problem solving, or stress management.

Ages and Stages in Mission Education

An effective educational program with a declared value of mission awareness and action takes into account ages and stages of readiness for mission. At each level of growth and development there are opportunities for mission education that are like pearls added one by one to a necklace. There are a number of books describing developmental characteristics of children and even life stages of adults. *On Behalf of Children* by Linda Isham and *The Teaching Church at Work,* both published by Judson Press, have charted and spoken to these concerns. Refer to them a you read the following mission program suggestions. See Appendix 1 for other resources.

Birth to One Year

The infant is dependent upon his or her parents for every kind of care. In this first year the foundation is built for whatever is to come emotionally, socially, physically, and intellectually. The church nursery is a place where parents and teacher can work together to create an environment where the infant feels safe. The child is cared for physically with food and clean, dry clothing and bedding. He or she is held and cuddled and given an opportunity to move and strengthen muscles. Intellectually the infant needs stimulation—things to look at, reach for, and listen to; someone who talks, sings, and hums to him or her. Socially and emotionally the infant needs to know that someone will respond to his or her cry. If the infant is cared for affectionately and his or her physical needs are adequately met, he or she learns to trust. If he or she is not cared for properly, or if inconsistency of treatment is the pattern in his or her early life, he or she will become fearful and will mistrust not only people and objects but him/herself as well.

The educational goal of the teaching church relating to infants is to provide an environment that fosters trust, with caring people who are knowledgeable about early childhood development. This atmosphere may be a continuation of the home situation, or it may be the only or best place where the infant receives this nurturing. The church nursery should be a place where all children experience holding, cuddling, patience, a sense of safety, affirmation, and love—whether they have experienced these feelings at home or have been deprived of them. The nursery is also the place where new parents can receive support, encouragement, and guidance. It is also a place for parents to experience a time-out from constant childcare. The teaching church must lay the foundation for future missioners in its care of the infant, the child, and the parents.

The nursery provides opportunities for mission to the whole family—not just the baby. Why not teach baby-sitting skills, parenting skills, and health care? Education and mission can be joint efforts as the congregation sets up and facilitates support groups for new parents, single parents, and teenage parents. The nursery is a good place to inform families about adequate day-care facilities—how to find the right one an what is available in your community. There is a need to inform families of nursery children about resources available to them in the community. Become aware of the level of child abuse in your community (even in your church) and explore ways you can educate and do mission in this area of concern.

Parents, grandparents, and siblings can learn new ways of relating to the child at home by helping in the nursery. The nursery staff that is concerned about follow-up care can include home visits and develop a working relationship with case workers, home health care and social service centers. The teaching nursery might be the place for new families to learn about nutrition help from Women, Infants and

Children (WIC) or about immunization clinics.

Group development experts state that trust is the basis for goal formation and agreement in groups, be it a task force, an education committee, a church board, a state cabinet, or a national defense committee. The teaching church, which is concerned about mission, is not a baby-sitting service but a network of information and of caring and loving people, acting now with the future in mind and fostering trust in God's children.

Nursery (Ages 2-3)

During a child's second and third year he/she learns to walk, talk, and coordinate movements. This is the time of exploration of the world as he or she experiences it. Consistent disciplinary techniques that encourage independence enable a young child to learn how to cope with later situations requiring choice, self-confidence, and autonomy. Inconsistent discipline, constant disapproval, and overprotectiveness tend to foster self-doubt in a child. The teaching church realizes that nursery age children are full of wonder in regard to all there is to see and touch and do in the world. Their first concept of God may be to hear that God created all these wonders. Contact with adults in the church helps young children experience a God-like love and build a positive attitude about the church. Young children are very sensitive to adult feelings, actions, and even unspoken attitudes. They notice how "big people" feel about the Bible, prayer, the environment, and even other adults. Young children are testing the rules and their own wants, asking questions over and over again. They are self-centered and tend to play near others rather than with them. Limits are important to young children. It's scary for a young child to think that he or she can get whatever is wanted simply by asking, screaming, pinching, or hitting.

A mission-oriented church provides the stability of a predictable environment for young children, allowing for exploration and discovery and offering loving guidance and encouragement that do not stifle natural curiosity. Attitudes toward all children need to be open and caring. Expectations of boys and girls need to be unbiased (some staff education in this area might be necessary). Resource materials need to consider inclusiveness of sex, age, race, and ability. The world is an exciting place for the young child, and this is a perfect time to offer a diversity of educational material, such as pictures, books, puzzles, toys, or music. Sharing is a big issue for children, and they need opportunity and affirmation for doing so. For some children it is difficult to be separated from parents, and their experiences at church can foster future confidence and security. All the support groups mentioned for parents of infants can be continued for parents of nursery children. Active two- and three-year-olds can bring joy and stress to parents. Parents ask, "What is normal?" and "What should I do?" Feedback from nursery staff to parents can build a network of encouragement and support. The two- or three-year-old child can learn in the nursery that "People are kind"; "I can do it"; "The world is safe—I will not be allowed to hurt myself or others, and they won't be allowed to hurt me"; "Church is a good place." Lessons such as these build self-confidence and self-esteem.

Kindergarten (Ages 4-5)

The four- and five-year-old is developing motor skills, and he or she may try riding a bike, building things, throwing a ball. A favorite expression may be: "I want to do it myself." This age child interacts with the environment, begins to play with others, is ready for small group games, and can take turns. Because many children of this age are in day care, nursery school, and play groups, their social world is expanding. They pick up words and behaviors from bigger children and adults and test them out for responses. Christmas is a very special season for children of this age. They identify with the baby Jesus, remembering their own and their siblings' birthdays. They know Jesus grew up to be a kind man—especially if they relate to kind adults in their world. The teaching church that encourages a child to participate in activities, to ask questions, and to play helps the child to initiate his or her own ideas and behaviors. The more experiences the four- or five-year-old is allowed to have, the more experiences he or she will try to have on his or her own. If we as a teaching church restrict the child's activity and inquisitiveness, he or she may be cautious, hesitant, and even guilty about initiating activities on his or her own. A mission-oriented church will stimulate the kindergarten child's environment by providing toys that encourage physical activity. Many churches provide outdoor recreational facilities, including swings, slides, climbing bars, and so forth. The church also invites the children to participate at their level of ability in service projects for people they know—coloring or drawing pictures, picking flowers, helping to pick up toys, passing napkins, holding the baby (with help), or telling a story. A young child develops strength, confidence, and courage to initiate ideas and actions for the betterment of the family, the community, and society when his or her initiative is affirmed by the parent, the teacher, and the church.

Elementary Age Children

From age six to eleven children become fairly competent at manipulating objects and events by themselves. Boys and girls (with equal encouragement) learn to make and build things, to study, to read, and to follow their interests. They look to adult models and then to peers for ideas, support, and encouragement. If encouraged by the adults in their lives, they develop a sense of industry and enjoy being curious and looking for answers. Without the support of adults, children may lose interest, be discouraged at their lack of success, and tend not to try or to complete future tasks. Children grow from self-centeredness to a concern for others, from concrete thinking to abstract thinking. They learn to generalize learnings. They form a relationship with the "real" Jesus, and after studying about him, they feel they can tell God anything. These years in a child's life within the teaching church are the ones of community building. Friendships are formed; extended families are nurtured; and peer groups become a source of growth and support. Children gain a sense of belonging. This aspect is particularly important in our highly mobile society. Many families relocate frequently and need the sense of belonging found in the church. Mission education recognizes each child's individuality, provides opportunities for learning about Jesus and heroes of the Bible, and offers guidance for acting out some of the Christian principles in their lives. Children can learn cooperation by working together on service projects.

A mission emphasis in church education may be reflected by the formation of clubs and groups for elementary age children, and through those groups the church may reach out to others who are not regular church attenders. The teaching church considers the need in its community for after school clubs, skill development clubs, boys' clubs, girls' clubs, recreation and playground facilities. Camping experiences enable children to learn and grow together with careful guidance. They can explore issues, grow in their own faith concepts, and expand their world together. Older children look to counselors and teachers as models, so careful selection and commitment of staff is part of the church's mission. This is a good time for visits from missionaries and community workers who can tell their stories and share their adventures. Shared experiences, such as doing service projects, learning as a group, making decisions, solving problems, singing, studying, and praying are building blocks for future adults as well as structure for growing children. Habits encouraged and formed now in response to God's calling often are lifetime disciplines that enrich and enable a Christian life of mission. Bible study appropriate for their age level and opportunities to question and relate biblical truths to everyday issues strengthen children's abilities to cope and give them guidance in their growing concern for fairness in their expanding world.

Youth

Those persons between the ages of twelve and eighteen are in the process of integrating all that they have previously experienced in order to develop a sense of self. They are changing physically and emotionally. They begin to ask themselves important questions: "Who am I?" "What do I want out of life?" "What do I believe?" Adolescents who can integrate their past experiences are better able to establish a clear sense of identity and move away from role confusion. The teaching church allows room for the questioning and searching that is part of this time in a person's life, recognizing that trying on different styles and roles is a way of finding a good fit. This is a time when the church reaches out to adolescents by providing opportunities for them to perform leadership roles both in their areas of skill and, with guidance, in areas that stretch and challenge them.

A woman who is a director of telephone hotline service for crisis situations related to the authors her story of growing up as a youth in the church. As a teenager she was representative for her denominational youth organization, helping to plan programs and provide leadership and speaking out on areas of concerns. The skills that she developed as a teenager eventually led to her career as an adult.

Another man told how at sixteen he was in drug rehabilitation and was given an opportunity to attend job corps leadership training. The skills that he acquired led to his current life work as a facilitator of community planning and action groups.

The teen years are a time when successes and failures are measured against questions of identity and/or confusion. Issues of teenage pregnancy, suicide, substance abuse, and employment opportunities must be assessed and responded to by the teaching church. The church can respond to the question "I think I know who I am, but how can I know?" by inviting youth to sit on boards, to try various leadership roles, to help plan and carry out local mission efforts, and to be part of a work camp or skill camp. The teaching church reaches out to youth who say, "Life's a bore; it's not worth it; I'll never get out of this town," by providing support groups skills training, recreation, listening and/or counseling services, family therapy, and affirmation.

The teaching church responds to youth who "have all the answers" with opportunities to try them out by participating in political activism, work camps, field trips, speaking/debating experiences, camps and conferences, youth conferences and committees, big brother/big sister programs, or by writing newsletters. This is a good time to invite youth to help plan their own mission education.

Youth want a safe place to talk and ask about ideas, skills, feelings, and behaviors. They value relationships with straight-talking adults who share personal experiences and support and care about youth.

College and vocational training and decisions about employment are issues faced by older youth. The teaching church can help by providing resources, career events, field trips to schools, or visits from people who can talk about available choices. Exposure to possibilities can change the lives of youth.

This is also the age when young people consider serving their country. The church can be active in helping youth to explore their options, to recognize their choices, and to look at how the options relate to their beliefs.

The mission-centered church also recognizes that the parents of youth need support. Even a parent who is knowledgeable about developmental characteristics of youth can feel rejected and hurt by the youth who is pulling away yet still needing loving support. The teaching church can provide a library and a referral service for youth and adults. Sometimes a family can be helped by being reminded of specific Scripture passages—the prodigal son, Jesus at the temple, and the ever-present "I'll follow you anywhere" love of God. The church can give youth the continuous reminder that regardless of what they choose to be or do, they already are members of the family of God and that God's love for each of us has and will stand the test of time, struggle, searching denial, and acceptance. God's love is one thing youth can count on. The challenge to the teaching church is to represent that promise to all persons, especially youth. As youth reach out to others, they learn more about themselves. Also, as youth feel more confident in their own lives, they are better able to reach out to others.

Young Adults

Developing relationships, building families, and establishing meaningful careers are all part of young adulthood. People who have achieved a sense of self-identity are able to form close relationships, to share themselves and their possessions with others. People who have never achieved this sense of identity may feel isolated. A generation ago society assumed that young people followed a set progression—dating, marriage, children. Today individuals are choosing a variety of lifestyles—single-parent families, childless couples, single adults, shared households, extended families, and adult children living with parents. Young adults are putting their skills, knowledge, beliefs, and wants into action. They are ready to establish careers, vote, and get involved in community issues. The teaching church may choose to support some young adults financially and emotionally as missioners in their work. It may support others through involvement in their secular issues and concerns as well as involve them in the church's issues and concerns. It may support a natural linking of older, wiser teachers with young, searching adults. New parents want the best for their children and therefore may be interested in the church school facilities and curriculum. This is the time to train them to be teachers. Support groups are needed for parents, singles, and couples, as well as multifaceted groups. Social gatherings provide opportunities for play, interaction, sharing of homes and lifestyles, and conciousness raising. The church needs to provide ways for young adults to explore avocations, to discover ways to do mission at work, and to make sense out of the hierachies of authority and bureaucracy. This may be the time to offer skill training in communications and relationship building. Some young adults are dissatisfied with their initial choices and need help sorting, healing, and rechoosing. Those who experience success early in their lives may need help maintaining a sense of balance and continuity. The mission church sees each person as a missioner and adopts an attitude of responsibility to support and challenge physically, emotionally, and spiritually. If these young adults grew up in a mission church, they will be trying out what they learned and looking to the church for support as it was promised.

Each church must assess its membership in light of its needs, resources, and outreach possibilities and develop an educational program that fits. A church may choose to sponsor a college chaplaincy ministry, a day-care center, low cost housing, a job placement agency, a drug rehabilitation and counseling center, or a program that teaches life skills or health education. All of these are home and outreach mission concerns for young adults who are trying to ground themselves in relationships with people, work, life, and God.

Middle-Aged Persons

This is a time when the individual must resolve conflicts with self and the external world and think about the future and the desire to contribute to the betterment of life. Choices made earlier in life may have led to fulfillment or to dissatisfaction. This is a time when some who have raised families and established careers may want to try something new or respond to inner callings that have been kept undercover. Others who have had a life of reaction to society may want to dig in and do something great for the world. It's a time when some adults are ready to become teachers or guides to younger adults.

Issues of middle-aged people are varied. Some face the empty nest syndrome; others reevaluate their marital situation. They may be responsible for the care of elderly parents or face the death of parents. Some may begin a second, third, or fourth career. This is often the time of life when people desire to break out of constricting patterns and structures and experience the drive to produce something or do something of value for the world. In a changing world, parents are struggling with the different values of their youth and adult children. They may also be learning how to be grandparents. Their bodies, which are showing signs of change and wear, may need more attention. The teaching church must find ways to relate to all these concerns.

Many middle-aged people are ready to share a mature faith with others. They can bring a stable quality to the teacher-student relationship. On the other hand, some middle-aged people want the opportunity to shake up and look again at their faith concepts, reaffirming some and reforming others.

The church can make available information about:

- care for the elderly
- health
- community needs and opportunities for service
- financial counseling
- retirement planning
- travel opportunities
- social events

The church has the opportunity to inform people about how they contribute to the betterment of life. For those who need to reestablish a sense of identity, trust, and intimacy, the church responds with caring, support, and friendship.

The church educational program may simply help people to recognize that what they are doing is mission. Many people do not realize that they are doing God's work in many ways. One woman always wanted to be a missionary but spent most of her life caring for her family. She never went away, but she cared for babies, nursed the sick, taught Sunday church school, served meals, mended clothes, comforted the grief-stricken, and in many ways missioned to those who needed her. At eight-six she was a model to many. People need to hear affirmation and expressions of thanks. The church can tell them that they are missioners

Older Persons

Older people enter a period of reflection, accept the past, and begin to come to a resolution with life. Some are satisfied with their lives. They feel unity with others and with life. Others who have experienced many failures and disappointments may feel despair. The teaching church meets these people where they are, ministering to them or being ministered to by them. The church must respond to all the life issues facing older people—health; how to contribute to the community; learning; financial concerns; loneliness; coping with the death of friends; relationships with family members.

People are living longer and many people are retiring early. The church needs to address issues of recreation, leisure, meaningful work or avocation, making new friends, moving, and living conditions. The church must take responsibility for education and consciousness raising about the aging process. The church can be aware of opportunities for mission to and by older persons and enable that mission to come into being.

People with Special Needs

The teaching church needs to plan mission to and education for people who have mental or physical disabilities. A mission education program is ready for all people created by God. We need to examine our physical facilities for accessability, our minds for openness and acceptance, our programs for inclusiveness, and our plans for flexibility.

3
Mission and Vocation/ Avocation

Vignette: The pastor of the Community Christian Church is an effective worship leader and liturgist. She is a student of both the Bible and church history. She functions more than admirably as a church visitor in the community and as a pastoral counselor. Her sermons are exciting. She writes for several publications and convenes groups of clergy and denominational leaders. She is active in both denominational work and ecumenical affairs. She is, in short, a good pastor. She will probably never be nationally acclaimed, but the people whose lives she touches and the congregations she serves will never forget her.

At the same time she is a member of a service club, serves on the advisory board to the county commissioners, is active in a political party in the community, is a United Way supporter and officer, along with being a sports enthusiast and a member of the community choir. She is known in the church community as someone who can get things done.

In the same congregation there is a layman who is a successful lawyer. Besides his usual professional work, he volunteers his services to individuals and nonprofit institutions. He belongs to a service club, is active in his political party, and serves on the planning and zoning board of his county. He is a member of an environmental organization, a sports enthusiast, a coach of a high school lacrosse team, a member of the historical society, and a member of the community orchestra.

The layman, along with all the rest he does, is active in the administration of his congregation and is active in both local ecumenical affairs and national denominational work.

He occasionally does visiting on behalf of the church. He helps in the leading of worship as a liturgist and has been know on occasion to both teach and preach. He is known in the church and the community as someone who can get things done.

If one met the clergywoman or the layman and did not know who they were or what they did, it would be a long time before anyone could distinguish between vocation and avocation in their lives. That is because they are persons who see the fullness of the creation and the kingdom and who are at home in both the work of the church and the work of the world. While the pastor is primarily responsible for congregational life and the layman is responsible for being part of a successful law practice, one could never guess which was which, based on the enthusiasm or the ability that they bring to their vocations and avocations.

Vocation and Avocation

The mission of the church is done in the vocations and avocations of the people of the church. Vocation and avocation come from the word *vocare,* which means "to call." Both vocation and avocation are callings. Normally we think of vocation as an activity that provides an income and avocation as an activity that pleases us or gives us a sense of satisfaction. For the Christian the concept of the call needs to include both vocation and avocation so that our productivity is thought of or measured not only in terms of goods and services for which we are paid but also in terms of goods and services for which we are not paid in money but for which we are paid in a sense of satisfaction.

Having a vocation and an avocation brings a sense of wholeness and well-being that prevents a person from being restricted to the narrow focus of life that says, "The most important thing in the world is my job, and the rest of the things that don't pay money are secondary." Persons who have a sense of wholeness and well-being about themselves and who view the world in a wholistic way are able to transcend the common boxing-in that too many people experience. These persons are able to indulge in many avenues of expression that make the world a better place in which to live.

In Western cultures there has traditionally been the negative idea that it is nonproductive to spend time on things that aren't of so-called primary importance for existence. In the Middle Ages, for instance, artists were often criticized because they were not producing a good that was necessary. Likewise the clergy were also considered unproductive since the value of service was not held very high during a time when the majority of people lacked many essentials for life. In our culture fewer and fewer people are needed to produce the goods that all of us use. There is a growing emphasis on services, aesthetics, and the arts. This reality helps us to minister in many places, both vocationally and avocationally. Few people in our churches need to spend all of their time just to make enough money to keep food on the table and a roof over their heads. Many of us are at a place in life where we can be involved in avocations as well as vocations.

There are three questions that we can use to test where we are in regard to our vocations and avocations and whether the contributions we make are limited to only one area or are a positive mix of both. The first question is "Who am I?" It is never fully answered, but until it is asked, we are not in a position to evaluate how our vocations and avocations intertwine. The second question is "What do I believe?" The belief implied has a wide range. What do I believe about people? about creation? about money? about the good life? about being a Christian? The third question is "What am I about?" or "What am I doing with myself and my life?" To the extent that one can mesh vocation and avocation, one is probably on the way to effective discipleship.

We are ready to be missioners when vocation and avocation are interrelated and not divided; when we do not need to spend all of our waking hours working for food, shelter, and clothing; and when there is time in life for the enjoyment of the arts and for involvement in hobbies and relationships with other people.

How can this happen? How can this be done? There are some ways that individuals and the church can help people come to the place where vocation and avocation are intertwined. We can be about mission through discipleship in our chosen work and in our chosen "nonwork," even though the nonwork sometimes is harder than our work.

Recognizing Gifts

The teaching church can help people discover and recognize their gifts and opportunities. The discovery of gifts sometimes goes with the discovery of opportunities. For too many of us, gifts and opportunities are not recognized. Sometimes we recognize opportunities, but don't believe we have the gift to use the opportunity wisely. While gifts and opportunities don't always go hand in hand, they very often do. For instance, if an outgoing person has a great deal of knowledge about a certain subject, sooner or later the person will have the opportunity during conversation to share the gift of knowledge.

The teaching church can be intentional about challenging people to recognize their gifts and to find opportunities to use them. Historically, in mainline Protestantism there have been denominational and interdenominational activities for which young people have been picked to participate in the affairs of the church and to receive training in the work of the church. Some of the outstanding leaders in Protestantism today were trained in these denominational or interdenominational programs. A significant weakness in today's mainline church is that neither ecumenically nor denominationally have we been able to continue this kind of training program. This program is different from the annual conventional gathering of many thousands of youth for worship and learning. A real challenge for the church today is to find young people who will invest the time and energy to discover both gifts and opportunities to lead the church in the days to come.

Developing Gifts

After people have discovered and recognized gifts and opportunities, there is some responsibility on the part of the church to help them develop those gifts and opportunities. This responsibility need not be feared. It is in itself a kind of mission. These gifts can be developed in the local church in three ways—in one-on-one encounter groups, in small groups, and in large groups using the educational program of the church. The teaching church can design many appropriate courses of study and/or action to help people either singly or in groups to develop gifts and opportunities. This can also be done in ecumenical settings such as a school of religion or special courses. The church can also provide opportunities for the development of gifts through relationships with nonchurch organizations. In many communities telephone hotlines offer programs of training that far exceed the quality of training that could be done on the limited basis within one congregation. Indeed, the training for telephone workers on helplines is often on par with graduate courses for counselor training. Some of the gifts developed include the gift of listening, the gift of becoming less judgmental, and the gift of helping people wrestle with their own great issues.

Some Characteristics of a Teaching Church

Any church with a vigorous ministry has some clear characteristics that mark its teaching. This is certainly true of a teaching ministry that is dedicated to helping persons become active in mission. Some church characteristics are:

1. Openness to Miracles

Perhaps this characteristic is the least mentioned because it is the least thought about, but it is the place where true believers are able to start. The Christian faith is based on a series of miraculous interventions, beginning with creation and culminating in the birth, ministry, death, resurrection, and ascension of Jesus of Nazareth. Miracles, however, continued as the wind and the fire of the Holy Spirit came to the church, and many of us have experienced miracles in our own lives as we take seriously the words of Jesus: "Whoever loses his life for my sake will find it." We do not need to discuss the definition of the word "miracle." Miracle is about us; it is experiential. Miracle is what one allows it to be in one's own life. It transcends the scientific explanation of the universe. Miracle is not a run-of-the-mill occurrence, and we are not to live idly waiting for miracles. Rather we should try to do God's work as if there would never be another miracle; we should be doing God's work as if there would never be another miracle; we should be doing God's work as if *we* are the miracle. The reason miracle must be taken into account is because it happens in the most unlikely ways, and we do well to live our lives knowing that there can be miraculous intervention at any time, which should prevent us from falling into despondency, despair, or depression.

2. Self-Knowledge

The teaching church has self-knowledge. The church needs to know who it is as an institution. Since the church is made up of people who are limited and not sinless, the church is flawed. But in knowing the mission of the church, the teaching church can be absolutely firm. In the teaching church's firmness the concern for justice may need to show healthy anger as an expression of love. The teaching church also has a ministry that is open-ended. We can be ready to start, modify, change, or stop ministry. We need not be bound by the past, locked into the present, or blocked out of the future. An open-ended ministry means keeping the good from the past, doing what is necessary in the present, and being ready to venture forth to do whatever is called for in the future. We know of one large church where if twelve members share the same vision for a project, program, learning setting, or justice issue, they automatically have permission to organize and begin working. Twelve people committed to a program or an issue automatically become a bonafide program of that congregation. Should the issue or the cause remain strong, they may also petition for funding from the church budget and for a permanent place in the church's organizational chart.

3. Inclusiveness

Striving for inclusiveness is a broadening experience for both the institution and the individuals who comprise it. It is critical that a teaching church value inclusiveness and try to model it to and through the congregation. While one of the grand hopes of Christians is that our world will ultimately be absolutely inclusive, we still need to recognize that not even churches are racially inclusive and that at this time in our society some communities believe that they cannot afford to be. If only the congregational leaders in black and white churches have caught the vision of inclusiveness, what happens to the people who have not caught the vision? There is no excuse for racially exclusive churches, but inclusiveness just for show is not what the gospel calls us to.

4. Knowledge of Human Development

Another characteristic of the teaching ministry as we help people deal with the concept of vocation and avocation related to mission is the taking into account of our ever expanding knowledge of human development. Chapter 2 has dealt with human development in detail. Paul talked about the appropriateness of milk for the newborn and the young in the faith and meat for those who are more mature in the faith. Current knowledge about human behavior helps us to direct ministry to where people are. In this way children are dealt with as children, not as small adults with adult concepts pared down to their level. Children are children and need to be respected and treated for who they are. Their needs and their gifts are different from those of adults. In the same way there are needs and gifts that are characteristic of youth, young adults, middle-aged adults, and older adults. A characteristic of the teaching ministry is to support persons no matter where they are in chronological age or in their faith journeys. Each generation has the right to explore issues of faith rather than to accept answers handed down by a previous generation. As James Russell Lowell put it: "New occasions teach new duties; Time makes ancient good uncouth." The right to question and to be supported in the questioning is critical for people of all ages to be able to grow in wisdom and in faith.

5. Sense of Wonder

Children are born with a sense of wonder and awe, and it takes a while before they learn to act in a more sophisticated manner. A solid teaching ministry helps adults retain or regain a sense of wonder and a sense of awe. Anyone who has stood on the edge of the Grand Canyon could be nothing but awestruck. A rainbow, a newborn child, a beautiful sunset, and thousands of other sights and sounds can stir our awe and wonder. The extent to which we hide this feeling also determines the extent to which we hide ourselves from the ways that the Holy Spirit can deal with us. It is important to help people retain the sense of wonder and awe in a wondrous and awesome universe.

6. Support for Venturing

Another characteristic of the teaching church is helping and supporting persons in venturing. The prophet Joel called it dreaming dreams and having visions. The venturing of the mind and the spirit is a wonderful aspect of human nature. Venture can lead to adventure—physical, mental, and spiritual—and the teaching church supports the spirit of venture and adventure.

7. *Showing God's Love*

Another characteristic is showing God's love at every level of development. This means supporting people as they grow and change self-esteem, abilities, physical development, and age.

Fifty years ago there was a particular small church that was family-oriented and neighborhood-oriented and that had a wonderful support base for all the people in the congregation—children, youth, and adults. Children were welcomed at the door of the Beginners Class and the Primary Class. Older children in the Junior Class were not only talked to but listened to. Dialogue was very evident in the Junior High Class and the Senior High Class. There were Children's Day programs. At their worst they were performances for the adults, but at their best they were wonderful times of learning and being involved in the life of the congregation. There were youth group activities and exciting Bible studies. In the midst of all these activities there was no undue pressure to be what one was not. Perhaps the most supportive and exciting parts of the life of that church were the many ways in which young people were challenged to develop and use their abilities at the evening services. The question asked most often was "How are you using your gift?" Tremendous support from older members of the congregation was experienced by those who were growing up in the church. Among the adults there was an ongoing concern for one another—concern for people's spiritual well-being as well as their physical well-being and their employment situations. The congregation was supportive of the pastor, and the pastor cared for the congregation.

Although the church had the visual ups and downs of congregational business and politics, the overall characteristic was that of support. It is true that life today is more complex and that the church has more complex challenges than it did half a century ago, but the fact remains that a support system is critical if we are to help persons internalize vocation, avocation, and discipleship in relation to mission.

8. *Understanding of Power*

Another characteristic of the teaching church is its ability to help persons to learn to deal with power and bureaucracy. If there is one place where Protestantism has not adequately dealt with the real world in our most recent history, it is in coming to terms with power. There has been some misunderstanding of the reality of power, the place of power, and the channeling of power. A number of books have been written on the subject, and we will deal with the issue briefly here.

Power is given to Christians by the Holy Spirit. Our power can be translated into work, and part of that work is also power of organization and institutional power, which includes such things as the power of money, prestige, and a positive press. It is not helpful to go through life believing that one is powerless, especially when we already have the gift of power. It is also not helpful to misunderstand powerlessness for meekness, lowliness, and holiness. Jesus was meek and lowly, but Jesus also claimed his power. Jesus was able to be righteously indignant when necessary and soothing and calm when necessary. Jesus knew when it was appropriate to use power.

There is power in bureaucracy. It is usually the kind of power that is able to wear down those who would challenge or use the bureaucracy. In training people or teaching people to be disciples in order to do mission, we need to help them to understand the reality of power so that they are neither being overwhelmed by it nor blithely denying the reality of it. Persons who don't take power seriously should think about how the dynamics of a group change when a new person joins. The power of the newcomer immediately changes the group from what it was into something else.

In a complex and organized society the church needs to help people affirm and use personal power. We also need to help people to understand the makeup and workings of institutions and how those institutions can be changed— even the institution of the church.

Jesus knew when it was time to be righteously angry and was particularly angry at those who had made religion a weight on the backs of the people. Indeed, Jesus saved his most critical comments for those who had the power and opportunity to help people find freedom but instead chose to bind them with even greater weights. Chapter 23 in Matthew's Gospel give a clear account.

9. Ability to Help People Develop Spiritual Skills

Many Christians say they want to be spiritual, but they often have no idea about what it means or about how they can become spiritual. To be spiritual is simply to be developing one's gifts and the qualities of life that are asked of those who follow Jesus. Spiritual skills are abilities that can be honed in order that a Christian may live a more effective Christian life. Spirituality is not being overly sweet, weak, or "wimpy." It is not being a doormat; it is not being always nice and never controversial. Spirituality is a series of strong qualities in life. The best way to develop spirituality is gradually, without being overwhelmed but being intentional in terms of what is to be done and how much time is to be spent. Success cannot come unless we take definite steps to foster the development of spirituality.

Following are some ways to develop spiritual skills:

Prayer is probably the most common and most powerful spiritual skill. Prayer is not asking God to do for us what we think God should do for us. Prayer is communicating with God, that is, sharing with God from the depths of our own souls and being open for the Spirit of God to speak to us. Jesus modeled many spiritual skills, and prayer was certainly at the head of the list. A prayer that is "neutral" and open to the Spirit is a prayer that can be answered for each one of us.

Meditation is like prayer except that it is more "laid back" and less directive. Meditation is often practiced regarding a single thought or a single purpose. Whereas prayer may be very much like conversation and the emptying of oneself, hoping to be refilled by the Spirit of God, meditation allows us to interact with the Spirit of God concerning a single notion or idea.

Spiritual retreat is growing in popularity and practice. Spiritual retreat experts can be recommended by pastors and church leaders.

Fasting is a biblical custom that has reemerged in current times. Fasting is not for everyone, and there are different types of fasts. Fasting is basically used to empty the body physically and cleanse it so that it can be refurbished spiritually. When people are fasting, they tend to be more open to the Spirit. Before anyone begins to get into serious fasting, he or she should consult a physician.

Bible reading is perhaps the easiest spiritual skill to develop. All it takes is time, the ability to read, and the availability of a Bible. Many Christians have never read the Bible completely. By reading three chapters a day and five chapters on Sundays, the Bible can be read in a year. For those who are not familiar with the Bible, it is not recommended to read it cover to cover, starting with Genesis and ending with Revelation. One could easily be stymied by the time one got into Exodus. Leviticus and Deuteronony are not easy reading either. Instead, the reader is advised to read all of the Gospels, then the book of Acts, the letters, and then Genesis, Exodus, Judges, the historical books, the minor prophets, the major prophets, Leviticus, Numbers, Deuteronomy, and last of all the apocalyptic books, which include Daniel and Revelation.

Bible study can be accomplished individually or in small groups. Lectures on the Bible can be considered also to be a part of Bible study, although the authors believe that Bible study should be a sharing of what biblical passages mean. The Bible is such a marvelous and mysterious book that it says different things to different people. One person's interpretation may vary at different stages of his or her life. Using some of the background work of biblical scholars may be helpful during Bible study, but one does need to know the biblical languages of Greek and Hebrew. One simply needs to take the time, expend the energy, get some extra resource books, and possibly gather two or three other persons.

Awareness of our world and of our culture is another spiritual skill. A Christian needs to be well read and widely read. Also one needs to be aware of ideas that are not only different but sometimes alien and even distasteful to us. It is helpful for us to find out about points of view that are different from our own.

Compassion and love for other people—especially those who are somewhat difficult to love—is another spiritual skill. Jesus was concerned about the mentally and physically ill and impaired. Loving those who are hard to like is a special challenge of Christians. Obviously an inclusive church would take into account the needs for these people both in the teaching and preaching ministries of the church and in the adjustment of the church's facilities. Several churches in the community can work cooperatively to provide a ministry to persons who have physical or mental disabilities.

The ability to give and take and share love in intimate friendships is also a spiritual skill. All of us need to cultivate a number of friendships with people who are non-judgmental, accept us as we are, ask us hard questions, but love us no matter where we are in our life journey.

4
Mission and Evangelism

Vignette: Two churches, First Church of the Expanding Suburb and First Church of the Slowly Dying Industrial City, have excellent pastoral and lay leadership. Deeply committed to evangelism and mission, both congregations have meaningful, stimulating worship, relevant educational programs, and community outreach. Both congregations are inclusive throughout, even in the highest leadership levels. Women, young persons, single persons, and people of all ethnic backgrounds are in places of high responsibility. Faithful financial support from the members keeps the churches from worrying about bills. Members from both churches have contributed to their communities and denomination. One church is growing significantly; the other is barely holding its own. Neither church is overly concerned with numbers, but both are aware of their growth patterns. Each congregation is committed to demonstrating the love and compassion of God in as many ways as possible, whether it adds to the rolls or not. Both congregations clearly see themselves as part of the whole church in the whole world. The future of one congregation seems destined for institutional largeness and maybe greatness as a leading church in the area and the denomination; the future of the other in terms of institutional survival is questionable at best. Each church models the gospel. *Both churches are faithful.*

Mission and Evangelism

The original concept of mission meant the sending of persons overseas to evangelize the heathen. It was initially done denominationally, not ecumenically. At the turn of the century optimism ran high that every nation would be converted and that the world would be brought to Christ. But with more than five billion persons in the world today and with the world population growing quickly, Christians become more and more of a minority. At the same time we continue to be more insightful about the meaning of the gospel and about what mission and evangelism mean in the context of the gospel.

Mission and evangelism go together. There is not one without the other. Mission includes evangelism—sharing the Good News of the world's redemption in Christ. Evangelism includes mission—working out in the world what the redemption means.

Mission is reaching out to others and into ourselves in whatever place or time, and with whatever resources we have available. Mission may be the sharing of a smile; the giving of recognition, food, or clothing; participation in political action; befriending the friendless; speaking out against injustice; teaching/educating; respecting a position; providing a job. Mission is recognizing a need and responding out of our faith to the call to love one another.

Evangelism is sharing the Good News; preaching the gospel; and telling and showing our story. It is communication of the Word (the intricacies of that communication call us to look at how people best receive what we have to communicate)—be it through actions, words, or the media. Evangelism is also an invitation to people to join with us as people of God; to be part of the fellowship of believers and to recognize and accept their rightful place as children of God.

We know that we must not only meet people where they are culturally, socially, politically, and philosophically, but also respect their position. The gospel is not presented in cultural dress with economic baggage or a condescending attitude. The gospel is presented as God's Good News to all people.

We also see mission and evangelism in a worldwide way. Need for the healing "balm of Gilead" are in us, around us, near us, and far from us. There are mission fields at home and abroad, and these fields are waiting for harvest. Problems differ and needs vary, but the gospel can meet them all. There was a time when the church in the United States was primarily concerned with sending messengers/missioners to faraway places with strange sounding names so that the "heathen" could be converted. Now some of the so-called "heathen" nations are sending messengers/missioners to the United States.

The church is strongest in places where it was allowed to belong to the people and become indigenous to their countries. For example, mainland China was a target of evangelism for many Christian groups. When missionaries were sent out or killed at the time of the Communist revolution in 1948, many feared that the church died. But those fears were unnecessary. The Spirit of God is not vanquished by armies of any ideology. The Spirit of God is not contained by an "ism." The days were dark, but the light of the gospel was not extinguished. Christianity could not be stamped out. Indeed, Christianity continues to grow, and the government of China today has had to modify its stance regarding religion.

Aspects of Mission and Evangelism

The China story has a number of lessons for us about evangelism and mission.

1. Ultimately, evangelism and mission are God's work—in full partnership with God's people
2. There is no authentic evangelism apart from mission, nor authentic mission apart from evangelism.
3. Persons have the right to say no and reject our efforts.
4. Evangelism and mission are modeled in leadership.
5. Evangelism and mission are a two-way street.

1. Evangelism and mission are God's work—in full

partnership with God's people. Since early in the history of the church there has been tension between the ideas of the power and sovereignty of God and the ability and responsibility of humankind. One concept says that God does everything; and because it is God's nature to know all things, all that could ever happen is known by God and thus decided so that the world of human beings is actually of little account. On the extreme other end of the spectrum is the concept that because humanity has free will, all responsibility rests on the shoulders of humanity and we must do everything within our power to evangelize and do God's mission in the world. Believing in the former is enervating, and subscribing to the latter is overwhelming. While biblical proof texts for both points of view can be found, each is an isolated concept. Much closer to the truth (as is so often the case in "ends of spectrum thinking") is the concept of partnership between God and the people of God. Surely God's power is beyond our full comprehension, but the creation is neither God's hobby nor toy. It is God's full-time concern, and God is continually active in the Holy Spirit. God has given great intellectual and moral capacity along with free will to God's people. So God turns over some power, for better or worse, to those made in the image of God. When we believe that we operate on our own or that our power is enough, we delude ourselves; but if we believe that God does everything and that we need to do nothing, we fool ourselves.

In the economy of God there would be no loss, no waste, no offal; but God does not force or enforce that economy. Instead, God empowers people to do what God would do and would have done. (Let there be no mistake here that the authors are discounting miracle—that intervention into the lives and affairs of people that is beyond comprehension. Miracle is for real; but it is not in the regular order of the everyday world. We do well to work as if there is no miracle, but to hope that there will be miracle. Evangelism and mission are almost always the ongoing daily products of people living and acting the life of faith.) This calls for taking seriously the fruits of the Spirit in our daily life and work. This means being grounded in strong faith and being faithful, doing one's best and letting God do the rest. The invitation to come to God is offered by God; often it is delivered by a person. Doing work is an act of faith by people, knowing that it helps others and honors God. When we come to realize that the world is vast, the problems many, the injustice pervasive, and the needs overwhelming, we also begin to understand the wonder of the gifts God has given us and continues to give. None of us must do it all or do it all alone. When Elijah said that he, only he, was the remaining faithful servant of God, he was informed by the Spirit of God that a great number were still faithful. All we must do is to be a faithful partner with God, doing as much as we can do as well as we can do it. While this notion comes as a great relief to the most compulsive, it is not meant to let the lazy off the spot of responsibility. Evangelism and mission go together; evangelism and mission are equally God's concern.

2. There is no authentic evangelism apart from mission, nor is there authentic mission apart from evangelism. Word of the Good News and work of implementing its meaning go together. To be sure, sometimes certain facets of the Christian life and work are overemphasized to the apparent disconcern of other facets. In the full, worldwide, gathered church, different groups have different emphases related to mission and/or evangelism. In the last analysis, everything fits together. This is not only true of the biggest picture; it can also be part of the smallest vista. God's word of welcome and love needs to be heard by all of creation while God's work of righting wrong, creating opportunity, and helping persons to be whole needs to be done. Having hope only for the next life is not sufficient. Having happiness in this life with no eternal hope is also a hopeless position. Jesus made it clear in the first formal sermon he preached (and the last in his home church) that nothing had changed so far as God's priorities from the time of Isaiah. Jesus declared that God had sent him to

> ". . . preach good news to the poor.
> . . . proclaim release to the captives
> and recovering of sight to the blind,
> to set at liberty those who are oppressed,
> to proclaim the acceptable year of the Lord."
>
> Luke 4:18-19

This is the wholeness of salvation. Here and now, then and there. To try to convince someone who does not know from where his or her children's next meal is coming that God is loving and caring will not be very meaningful. Providing that next meal in God's name gives a more realistic reference point. Doing mission allows us ultimately to speak for the One in whose name we do the mission. There are differences about how "up front" or "laid back" the missioner should be, but that is a stylistic question that is related to the personality of the doer, for there is no fixed formula for where mission work ends and evangelism work begins. Some would say the words while doing the work. Some would allow the work to be its own word until the question is raised by the recipient of the work. Announcing God's love and grace and inviting persons to accept it is an age-old style of evangelizing. It can be done directly in a large group, such as a large evangelistic service. Billy Graham crusades typify this approach. The announcement can also be made in one-on-one setting, the people being strangers or friends. Radio and television have made it possible for the speaker who is making the announcement to be unknown and far away.

Because God makes every person different, many different types, styles, and nuances of the announcement are valid. Wonderfully different persons will respond in wondrously different ways to both the work of the kingdom and the verbal invitation to be a part of it. The questions of word and work (Which is more important? How should they be used?) can all be answered in the willingness of the people of faith to do what they do best, knowing there may be more yet to learn and do and not judging the different or even similar word and work style of others who are also committed to extend the kingdom of God. Those who are not against us are our helpers.

3. Persons have the right to say no to us and reject our efforts. Near the close of his ministry when Jesus looked at Jerusalem, he was greatly disappointed because of the rejection of his messsage. In a moving description of concern and compassion he talked of taking them under his wing as a hen with chicks (anyone who has watched a hen care for her chicks sees the fitting allusion to safety). Although most people experience some rejection of self or ideas early in life, they are never able to accept rejection without disappointment. All people have free will—the right to choose wrong, to not choose right, to choose poorly, or choose by refraining from making a choice. This is important to remember when our most compassionately based actions of goodwill are rejected. Not everyone is appreciative of hearing words of good news. Not everyone is able to be a good receiver of the word of mission. The reasons for saying no—or not saying yes—are as variegated as the persons to whom our word and work is addressed. It is their *right* to be wrong! The work we do and the word we speak is a responsible result of our having heard the word or been impressed by the work heretofore in our own lives. But many of us did not respond the first time we were confronted. So when people do not respond immediately, our responsibility is to continue to be faithful in our endeavor. Sometimes we don't speak the invitation of God's love clearly enough or lovingly enough, and sometimes our work is lacking in some way. But even when we speak the words clearly, lovingly, and compellingly and do our work successfully according to every criteria for planning, execution, and evaluation, there are many times when to be unheard and the work seems unappreciated. Jesus' parable of the sower and the different quantities of harvest is supportive of us here.

No word that is spoken or no work that is done is without value. Although there are the last drops of water that fill the bucket, all the other drops in the bucket are equally as important. Paul helps us here in reminding us that there are different roles and different gifts, all of which work together to bring wholeness to God's kingdom. For those who are faithful there is no such thing as failure. Failure is a short-term, human concept. A long-term evaluation by kingdom values shows only success. Faithfulness will always be rewarded. One of the difficulties of the human condition, especially in our Western culture, is the "quick fix" syndrome. "Fast," "hurry," "now," and "quick" are words that are both descriptive and normative for too many of us in our society. The saints, however, need only to be told about the continuity of God's business. They do the best they can in the present, trusting in God's Spirit for whatever else is appropriate. (Paul calls all people in the church saints. The authors choose the word here as a reminder of how highly Paul regards us.)

A "no" is a fair response for those who are not ready to say yes. They will be dealt with again, differently, until their yes is an honest decision or response to God's Word and/or work done by us on God's behalf.

4. Evangelism and mission are modeled in leadership. To the extent that we as sayers and doers, evangelizers and missioners, are able to replicate what we say and do in the words and actions of our own lives, we are models. Persons who embody in themselves what they say and believe, make their words and acts more believable. The person who speaks eloquently of God's love and who is loving is a kind of proof of that statement. The person who does good works out of geniune love for persons is a proof of the good works.

It is true that all of us have feet of clay and imperfect and impure desires. We should not take ourselves too seriously, and we should certainly not believe that we are unusually holy or sin resistant. We can also be as intentional as possible in living (saying and doing) the Christian life so that our example is as positive as possible. After people get to know us well, our "clayness" will be apparent, but by then they will better know and understand the truth of the gospel—that all have come short of God's glory and that everyone stands on equal ground at the foot of the cross.

5. Evangelism and mission are a two-way street.
When Jesus was before Pontius Pilate, the tremendous pressure of the event prompted Pilate to raise a great cosmic question: "What is truth?" Many of us believe that Jesus is the Truth, but the meaning of the word varies. Truth is slippery! It is more than facts and science. It can be arrived at but never fully known. It is both constant and changing. When people of faith engage in evangelism and mission, they are operating out of a truth that is known to and believed by them. Sometimes, the perception called truth gets stuck and stale. It is not a case of becoming false; rather it is a case of more being added. We not only need to speak and do evangelism and mission, we also need to listen and let others do to and for us. None of us knows so much that there is nothing to learn. None of us is so strong to give that we need never receive.

The pastor who "gives all" to the congregation without caring for his or her own body, spirit, and mental health does a personal disservice. Jesus took time to refresh and renew himself, and a pastor likewise needs "away time" for refreshment of body, spirit, and mind. The church school teacher who has decided that he or she knows exactly what the biblical message means in regards to the class being taught may short circuit the work of the Spirit for both the class and himself or herself. The really good news of God's love is that we can give and receive.

Because life is an unfolding experience, our perception and understanding of the gospel grows (or should grow) as we grow. Those new in the faith need the milk of the gospel, but ultimately we need the meat of the gospel. (Vegetarians please note that this is from the apostle Paul who was trying to make a point, not supporting consumption of meat.) We have lessons to learn from people of faith (those less mature and those more mature than ourselves). We also have lessons to learn from those of no faith. Some of the most caring, compassionate, and helpful persons claim no allegiance to Christ or church, but they model Christian attitudes and action so beautifully that we can learn from them. In some cases until we can really hear and be open to the work of those we want to evangelize, we won't have the

The Church and Corporate Mission
Church Calendar for the Month

Sunday	Monday	Tuesday	Wednesday	Thursday	Friday	Saturday
1	2	3 monthly meeting Church Women United	4	5 weekly meeting Neighborhood Church Cluster	6	7
8	9	10	11 quarterly meeting Denominational Women	12	13	14
15	16	17	18	19	20	21
22	23 monthly meeting County Ecumenical Agency	24	25	26	27	28
29	30	31				

A Page from a Pastor's Desk Pad Calendar

Sunday	Monday	Tuesday	Wednesday	Thursday	Friday	Saturday
1	2	3	4 weekly breakfast with clergy from neighborhood	5	6 morning basketball with area clergy	7
8	9 monthly meeting area denominational clergy	10	11	12	13	14
15	16	17	18	19 monthly luncheon & program area ecumenical clergy	20	21
22	23	24	25	26	27	28
29	30	31				

capacity to speak and act in such a way as to have them take seriously our words and work. This is easier to see in family life, where parents and grandparents learn or relearn many lessons of life from children and grandchildren.

In the old days the process for growing in the faith was called "sanctification." More recently the term "transformation" was used. A common word today is "wholeness." The three words all refer to the concept of becoming what and who our potential is with the aid of the Holy Spirit. The term does not matter, but the growth is important. As we grow in grace, we may change our ideas about evangelism and mission. We are able to grow and change as we are open to consider new ideas. We can see the kingdom of God in larger terms. We can travel the two-way street of growth by saying and doing and hearing and being done unto.

The sample calendars may not be appropriate for all congregations and pastors, but they are indicative of "what is" for some and "what might be" for others. Almost every congregation and clergy who understand the rudiments of corporate mission find themselves involved in it at the local level.

Corporate mission is working together with another church or churches to accomplish a specific task. Personal mission can also be a part of the corporate mission. The church calendar and the pastor's calendar give some clear indication about belief in the corporateness of the church based on corporate/personal involvement in it.

Brief History

From the earliest history of the church, beginning with the unlikely and disparate group of twelve disciples, there was a push and a pull. Jesus prayed that all would be one in faith.

> "I do not pray for these only, but also for those who believe in me through their word, that they may all be one; even as thou, Father, art in me, and I in thee, that they also may be in us, so that the world may believe that thou has sent me" (John 17:20-21).

5
The Church and Corporate Mission

P aul dealt with this theme in his letter to the Ephesians:

" . . . eager to maintain the unity of the Spirit in the bond of peace. There is one body and one Spirit, just as you were called to the one hope that belongs to your call, one Lord, one faith, one baptism, one God and Father of us all, who is above all and through all and in all" (Ephesians 4:3-6).

Human beings that we are, we have both coalesced and broken apart. The church was a single entity until 1054 when the east and west, Constantinople (Orthodox) and Rome (Catholic) officially separated. Only in the very recent past has there been a face-to-face meeting of the Eastern Orthodox patriarch and the Roman Catholic pope after more than one thousand years. Following the east and west split, the Western world saw the Anglican church come into being. The Reformation was the next major breaking apart of the church. This was followed by the rise of the Free Church, Mennonites, and Baptists. As time passed there were more divisions, splits, and groups. The twentieth century in the United States has seen a myriad of new churches—some Pentecostal, others Baptist, independent, fundamental, and so forth. Today, while a number of mainline denominations are involved in bilateral and trilateral discussions on unity and possible union or reunion (that is, two denominations or three denominations talking with one another), while the Orthodox and Roman Catholics reach out to each other, and while there are ecumenical efforts at every level of organization from local to international, there are at the same time many examples of cutting off and dividing away and refusing to interact or be together. This refusal to interact is sometimes based on personality traits and differences. Other times it is based on theology and/or doctrine, nationalism, economics, or partisan politics. A few years ago a pastor was invited to an ecumenical meeting of clergymen, but he attended only the "professional" part of the meeting, after the Bible exposition and prayer time was finished, because he would not worship with clergy from other denominations! We are all one, whether we like it or not, believe it or not, act on it or not. The mind of God is not changed about unity by any action or lack of action by God's people.

The biblical material on unity is one driving force for corporate and cooperative mission. Another force is simple common sense. Because of history and position in life, background and understanding, different people are drawn to different expressions of faith in a myriad of denominations. Those denominations are attempts to be faithful to God in corporate mission, and many work at cooperative mission even beyond their own denominational framework.

Unity Around Home

To be sure, unity does not compel union, at least in the present or near future. Unity is a matter of the Spirit (invisible), while union is physical, organic, structural (visible). Even where there is union that is structural and visible, there is not necessarily unity. It is easy to understand this dichotomy in terms of marriage or deep personal friendship; the strength of a solid marriage or friendship is based on the synergism or coming together of the strengths of both parties. It can be equally true in the religious realm, although it is less simple to comprehend.

To be involved in corporate mission we begin by affirming oneness and unity. The oneness and unity is a shared faith in the message of the Good News of the gospel to and for all creation. Uniformity is not called for nor required. The unity crosses theological and doctrinal lines, personality

differences, structural types, and denominational idiosyncrasies, such as mode of baptism, use or nonuse of creeds,
and use or nonuse of liturgy. It is joyous assent to God's love.
We continue involvement in corporate mission by doing
something. The occasional interdenominational, ecumenical, or interfaith service is an important early step and foundation for greater cooperation in the future. The
community Thanksgiving service is an interfaith expression
of thanksgiving for personal and national blessings and a
good starting place for other cooperative efforts. Study
groups are important also. Learning about one another
helps us develop keener insights about our own history and
experience. Action programs are corporate mission. With
clearly stated, achievable goals these programs help build
the foundation for more corporate mission action. When
the religious community decides to raise a certain amount
of money on a certain day for a specific purpose, such as a
CROP walk, it sets the stage for even more effective mission.
An exciting resource on ecumenical and interfaith cooperation is a book entitled *Local Ecumenism and Interfaith
Cooperation*[1] published by the Graymoor Ecumenical Institute. This is an updated and revised edition of *Parish Ecumenism*, which was first published in 1976. It contains
several hundred items of local ecumenical interest, programs, and suggestions for ecumenical activity at the congregational level. The resources and suggestions are drawn
from many different traditions and experiences to empha-
size that we can and do learn from one another. It encourages the interaction that has as its final objectives the unity
of the local Christian community and a deeper understanding, appreciation, and respect for the beliefs and traditions
of other faiths. Each chapter is followed by further suggestions and resources. The book also contains a selected bibli-
ography and glossary of terms. The chapter titles are:

[1]To order send $5.00 (plus 50¢ postage and handling) to Graymoor Ecumenical
Institute, Garrison, NY 10524.

Parish Ecumenism and Interreligious Dialogue
The Role of the Clergy
Beginning Grass-roots Ecumenism and Interfaith
   Cooperation
Ecumenical Education and the Search for Interfaith
   Understanding
Spiritual Ecumenism and Worship
Ecumenical Social Concerns
Local Ecumenical Dialogue
Covenants Between Local Congregations
Ecumenism and the Young
Interreligous Dialogue and Cooperation

The Lund Principle

The Lund Principle, which is a statement that came out of
an ecumenical conference in 1925, calls churches to do as
much together as possible except when a matter of principle
would be denied by being together or working together. For
instance, some groups could work, pray, and even worship
together, but not celebrate Communion together. This
was/is a matter of principle. Some denominations do not
allow nonmembers to receive Communion. Wherever a
group or individual follows the Lund principle, there
should be openness to the Spirit to examine ways for moving to more cooperation and more significant expressions of
unity. To this end, intentionality is a key. Happenstance,
vagary, and procrastination promote neither unity nor the
kingdom of God.

Jesus' ministry was Spirit-guided, wisely planned, and
judiciously executed. The next chapter deals with the concept of planning for ministry. Often denominations offer
guidelines for cooperation based on doctrine, theology,
practice, opportunity, and need. There are concrete examples of cooperative ministry at the international, national,
state, regional, local, and neighborhood levels. The examples include worship and work. The World Council of
Churches distributes food in famine areas. The National

Council of Churches publishes educational materials. State ecumenical agencies run disaster-relief networks. Services at regional, local, and neighborhood levels include care for the homeless and hungry. All the groups worship and pray. If there are any areas considered forbidden or tentative, denominational leaders will note them along with reasons.

Corporate mission is most visible and most easily done at the local level. Usually a particular need is met by a regular, planned effort. For instance, the resettlement of refugee persons and families has often been done by a group of congregations in a community. If a family is burned or flooded out of its home, nearby churches often cooperate to respond quickly. Needs are assessed, and resources are calculated and committed. Usually both short-term and long-term solutions are decided. One problem is evident: The greater the distance between us and the need, the more difficult it is to be so intentional. But other needs—those that we don't see or experience so vividly—also deserve attention on an intentional, planned, or corporate basis.

In order to be the church in corporate mission, the people and the congregation need to know who they are, including their history and their hope. What are peripheral matters and what are unbending core principles need to be discerned.

The Christian imperatives of sharing the Good News and helping those in need can be honored without selling out heritage or future. There is also the imperative to do good for those in need based on a common humanity—irrespective of what theology we bring to "common humanity." The Christian imperative drives us to cooperative Christian and interfaith action.

Needs to be addressed may be local or global, simple or complex, or maybe almost impossible. The most distant and complex global needs are often addressed by the outreach agencies of religious and secular organizations, which need money, prayerful support, and sometimes direct, hands-on help.

It is helpful to remember that many of church members are already involved in mission outside of the church. Through both secular organizations and personal involvement, these people affiliate with and relate to hundreds of good causes supporting justice and equity. Volunteerism is unique to the United States. Volunteerism is acknowledged by public policy and the federal tax code. The Internal Revenue Service encourages contributions to religious and charitable organizations by granting them tax-exempt status. This means that a gift by an individual or corporation to a tax-exempt organization can be a tax deduction for the person or corporation.

Corporate mission is as extensive as the needs addressed by those who care. For members of a particular congregation, expressions of involvement in corporate mission include but are not limited to:

- local church activity, such as teaching and visiting;
- volunteerism, such as being a school crossing guard, visiting the sick, working for United Way or service clubs;
- membership in secular organizations for the arts, environmental concerns, or historical preservation;
- membership in political parties in which one tries to reflect Christian values and ideals in the democratic process.

Churches also show institutional concern through their budgets and programs. Even with our members doing worthwhile tasks, it is important for congregations and the larger associations to budget and program for study and action. This includes our denominational and ecumenical organizations. Budget lines and programs are a sure insight into what we are about.

The Church and Politics

Whenever there is a question of church involvement in justice issues, the word "politics" usually follows. It is not usually said kindly or knowledgeably. Many issues are political without being partisan. No political party can claim concern for justice as a private goal. If an issue becomes partisan, it is not because the church addresses it, but because others have already taken sides.

In our democratic country all citizens have the responsibility and right to be engaged actively in politics, including partisan politics. The church only intrudes into politics for goals of justice, fairness, and equity. We have a constitutional right and biblical and moral imperative. So long as the religious community focuses clearly on issues and does not support particular parties or candidates, there can be no danger from formal governmental backlash. Indeed, there is more risk of internal strife than of external pressure.

Perfection in terms of handling difficult issues can be as illusive for the religious community as it is for other institutions. Criteria for judgment of others should include gentleness and mercy, but it is not fair to judge others more harshly than we judge ourselves. To seek to do justice, even if it is done imperfectly or without success, is surely better than not to seek to do justice at all.

It is not always appropriate to wait for a better time to get involved in mission. Some are called to be out front, calling for others to follow. The high cost of involvement should not stop us. When a group honestly wrestles with the troubles of our time, the Spirit will manifest itself, and clarity will come as we are willing to be challenged and respond. In the United States the involvement of the church in issues such as slavery, child labor, and the right of persons to organize for collective bargaining is proof that the Spirit leads when the church responds. In the last analysis, those who live, walk, and work with the Spirit can count on gentle, loving, merciful judgment from God.

6
Planning for Mission

Vignette: For some it is on the refrigerator door; for others on the bedroom mirror; yet others have it on the desk; some carry it in a briefcase or pocketbook or shoulderbag; still others carry it in a shirt pocket or jacket pocket; for some it is carried in the mind. For almost everyone there is some form of calendar There are short-term calendars to plan the upcoming day; there are mid-term calendars to plan this year's vacation and holiday schedule; and there are long-term calendars to plan a career or a family. Many people make decisions without conscious awareness that they are planning. Humankind has been planning informally throughout history. Only recently has planning become so popular and important that courses are offered and innumerable articles published about it. These confirm planning as part of a life process. Planning is not a recent invention or discovery; it has always been seen as a valuable tool for saving time, energy, and money. From the simplest one-day personal plan to the most complex twenty-year corporate plan, the goal is to make life easier, less cluttered, and more meaningful. Planning helps us to do our best—whatever we do.

So far in this book we have seen how the teaching church is active in mission in a number of ways. Chapter 1 defines "missioner" and the role of the church. In it we are reminded of our history and our call to mission. Chapter 2 helps us look at the way we educate for mission. Chapter 3 challenges us to look at ways the church can help people recognize and do mission through their vocation and also through avocation. Chapter 4 differentiates between mission and evangelism and challenges us to do both. Chapter 5 emphasizes corporate mission and ways in which churches can be active, both denominationally and ecumenically. And now in Chapter 6 we will explore reasons and ways to plan for mission. In all these areas planning will lead to demonstrable accomplishment.

The Planning Process–An Overview

For people of faith and for the religious community, good planning can enable mission. Planning is not an end in itself; planning is not the mission; planning is not a god but a guide. Planning is a valid and valued tool for mission and mission strategy. Many churches already have some form of planning and planning process. For those who are in the early stages, a simple 1–2–3 description of the planning process is found in three questions:

1. What do I/we want to accomplish and when?
    WHAT IS THE GOAL? (include TIME)
2. How can it be done?
    WHAT IS THE PLAN?
3. What will it take?
    WHAT ARE THE RESOURCES?

A Planning Process

Different planning experts and different planning models use different words, but all planning models include moving toward a goal by using available resources.

A typical planning guideline might look like the chart on the following page .

Planning and People

Churches do well to remember that the "going" is as important as the goal. The goal is where we want to end up, but we do not *use* people to arrive at goals. We *involve* people in setting goals, developing strategies, eliciting resources, and using plans of action. The religious commu-

Goal or purpose:

Program plan:
    What is supposed to happen?
    Who will make this happen?
    When will this happen?
    Where will it happen?
    How will it happen?
    What will be different?

Criteria for evaluation:

Program manager:

Resources needed:

    Time:
    Funds:
    Other:

Special comments:

nity shows and proves its values by sticking to those values in all facets of mission, including the planning process. Goals can be set as part of the planning process for the total program of a church. Goals can be set for all the different parts of a local program, including not only the in-house program but also the denominational, ecumenical, and interfaith cooperative program.

It is important that a broad base of members affirms the principle of planning and engages in the process of planning. Once a plan is developed and approved, it should be reviewed and evaluated on a stated time basis. Sometimes, upon evaluation, a plan needs simply to be worked at more diligently; other times it may need to be amended and modified. Maybe it was too shallow and undemanding, or perhaps it was too idealistic and impossible. The plan needs to be reasonable and the work doable but not so simple as to lack in challenge or so difficult as to be overwhelming.

Beginning the Planning Process

A planning process can be in at least two ways. One way raises the question "If there were no program in place for this organization, what would we want to put in place?" This is planning from scratch. Another way to approach the planning process is to ask these questions: "What are things we do now that, even if we don't do them well, we would not be willing to give up? What else should we plan to do?" This implies some evaluation of current missioning before planning occurs. Actually, evaluation is part of the planning process, either before the planning process and/or after the planning process.

The planning process is dynamic and is a vehicle for the Spirit of God. People who think, dream, evaluate, and strategize are often more open to visioning and seeing possibilities that were of unthought of before or thought to be impossible. This is a good reason to include as broad a spectrum of membership as possible in the planning process. Church board and committee members and other members of the congregation should be included.

Evaluating

Those who have responsibility for carrying out the planned programs should also participate in the evaluation of them. Evaluation takes into account both plus and minus factors related to the allocation of resources.

Failure to reach a goal is not seen as either a personal or a systems failure. Not reaching a goal has a reason. When the reasons are known, the goal can be modified or dropped. Sometimes goals are too ambitious and simply cannot be reached. The failure here is in the setting of the goal, not in the ability to reach the goal. For instance, one local church set a large increase in membership as a goal, but the community's population was decreasing and the remaining residents were already church members. The failure was in the goal, not in the implementation.

Evaluation is not designed to blame or shame; it is a check and balance, a way to improve future plans, a way for implementers to learn and resource future plans; it is designed to keep a plan on track or to retrack it. The key question for evaluators is WHY—Why did we succeed? Why did we not achieve our goal? Often the learnings from honest evaluation are helpful to other segments of the life and program of the institution.

Getting Started

Because we walk before we run, it is usually wise to start a formal planning process in just one or two facets of the life of the church. The plans can be quite simple but should exemplify the total planning process. Following are three sample plans: one is for participation in alleviating world hunger; another is for a program of visitation within a congregation; the third is for a new mission thrust.

The first chart may at first glance appear to be too large a vision and program. In fact, it helps persons to learn that big problems are often solved in a variety of ways and in small pieces. The data on world hunger is available. Causes are complex and solutions difficult, but this congregation is doing its part to learn and act. The program is clear and doable. Checkpoints are discernable. At the end of the program, the congregation evaluates its progress and effectiveness.

A Global Mission Concern

Goal: Hunger in the world will be diminished in 19__

Program: Members of the congregation will be given opportunities to help alleviate hunger.

Program plan details:
  What is supposed to happen?
    Hunger in the world will be alleviated.
  Who will make this happen?
    Members of the congregation.
  When will this happen?
    Through ongoing opportunities throughout the year.
  Where will this happen?
    Worship, study, small groups, special groups, and specific programs.
  How will this happen?
    Members will study the issue, set congregational goals and personal goals, support denominational and other specific programs.
  What will be different?
    Some persons will be better fed; the world hunger problem will be somewhat lessened.

Criteria for evaluation:
  Was the program carried out?
  How many persons participated?
  How much help (money) was generated?

Program manager: Chairperson of mission board (or similar group in the congregational structure).

Resources requested: $200 for educational material.

Congregational Care Program 19___

Goal: Each member of the congregation will be visited during the next year.

Program: Each family unit will be visited in the setting of their choice two times this year.

Program plan details:
    What is supposed to happen?
        Each family unit is to be visited two times during the year.
    Who will make this happen?
        The visitation committee will be responsible for making the visits or have the visits made.
    When will this happen?
        Throughout the year (completed by January 19___).
    Where will this happen?
        In the setting of the family unit's choice (usually the home).
    How will this happen?
        Every family unit will have received two planned visits this year.

Program manager: Chairperson of the visitation committee.

Resources requested: $100 for material for visitor training.

In this planned program the details are clear. The training of visitors will be another program plan. This program would be evaluated at every meeting of the visitation committee, with the chairman reporting to whomever has ultimate responsibility.

The preceeding examples are relatively commonplace. They put into very concrete settings plans that many of us carry in our minds. They unify the focus or plans of a number of individuals in order that all are working together in agreement and understanding of a stated goal. It is in areas such as new mission and ministry and new ventures of faith and endeavor that a formal planning program is critical. An "end state" is the desired result. The program plan details specify time, resources, place, and persons to reach the end state. Criteria for evaluation will help keep the goal in the minds of those responsible for its implementation.

An example of new mission follows.

Ministry to Homeless Persons in Our County (19___)

Goal: Two hundred homeless people will be aided in our county this year.

Program: The county government will coalesce resources of government and private agencies to serve at least 200 homeless persons this year.

Program plan details:
What is supposed to happen?
At least 200 homeless persons will receive aid this year, the aid to come from and be focused by the county government.
Who will make this happen?
The county, with help from the nonprofit sector and at the insistence of the religious community, including this church.
When will this happen?
Through the year, especially in the most difficult weather.

Where will this happen?
Throughout the county in appropriately chosen settings.
How will this happen?
The county government and nonprofit agencies (including the religious community) will study the situation, recommend action, and provide funding.
What will be different?
At least 200 homeless persons will have their basic needs met.

Criteria for evaluation:
Did county government accept the lead role?
Did other agencies and churches help?
Was the issue studied?
Were at least 200 homeless people served?
If not, why not?
What helped/hindered goal accomplishment?

Program manager: Chairman of the committee on community relations.

Resources requested: $1,000 and 5 volunteers to be trained for the program.

When a church is ready to get involved in mission, such as helping the homeless, good intentions go farthest when organized and systemized. Many of us could help one, two, or even several homeless persons. But when an issue is as large and complex as the issue of homelessness, it demands cooperation and a wide range of resources. The church that formulated the goal was wise. Although it volunteered its money and people, it also recognized that a major problem needed a major response and that the county government could best pull the resources together and focus them. Too often people of faith see a hurt, an issue, or a problem that appears to be overwhelming. We wring our hands and cry out in anguish when we could better reach out our hands to other resources and call out for help. We don't need to do it all. We need start working toward a solution.

Concluding Unapologetic Postscript

In the book of James we are, in effect, told that to see someone in need and simply say, "Good luck" or "Have a nice day" is not enough. We are called to believe and to act. Action for justice is the frontier for mainline churches today. Each denomination has a few prophets, and most congregations have many concerned persons; but justice issues within the community often seem too complex for us to deal with.

Simple intentional planning will get us started and give assent to Jesus' statement "As you have done it to the least of my brothers and sisters, you have done it to me."

Different congregations will find themselves at different places regarding teaching and mission. All will have some clear strengths. Many will have some clear weaknesses or areas for mission that have been overlooked. The planning process—formal or informal— can be used to begin a mission program or to build up places where there is a weakness in the program.

A helpful exercise, after studying this chapter, would be to evaluate strong points of the congregation's mission; then think about some weak spots and work on a planning process to address them.

Appendix 1

Study Guide

To enhance your use of this book, the authors have delineated a plan for study and action. Use it as a starting place for your church. Then explore other ways to use the book and to clarify and implement your mission.

1. The pastor(s) and mission committee members should read the book.
2. Discuss the possibilities and implications of an evaluation of missions by all church members.
3. Formulate a plan for introducing and implementing a total church mission exploration.

Example:

a. After all church members study chapter 1, they can discuss and explore their church history and come to a clear definition of mission for individuals and the congregation.

b. Individual boards or committees study chapters that speak directly to their emphasis:

Board of Christian education—Chapter 2
Board or committee of evangelism—Chapter 3
Interfaith committee—Chapter 5
Board of deacons—Chapter 6

c. At the same time individual boards and committees study and clarify their roles, they need to meet together regularly as a whole body to educate one another and stay together in the search and discovery process.

Example: The board of Christian education decides that from early childhood on, the education program will include local outreach. At the same time the board of evangelism identifies a neighborhood that is in need of outreach. A coordinated effort may evolve as a result of a unified understanding. Newsletters, bulletin boards, mutual goal setting, reports during worship time—all these factors keep people active in the study and planning process.

    d. When the exploration and discussion process reaches its fruitfulness, ask boards and committees to present recommendations to the mission committee.

    e. The mission committee's job is now to correlate and integrate these recommendations and to present them to the church body for comment, question, understanding, and action.

    f. The goal of the study is to

- decide how you want to act on that declaration by (1) naming what mission you are now doing, and (2) deciding what you want to do in the future in the name of mission
- set goals
- establish a plan
- communicate your decisions and plans
- implement action
- evaluate mission

Following is a chapter-by-chapter series of questions and study suggestions. Consider inviting resource people to guide, stimulate, and affirm your actions

Chapter 1 The Role of the Church in the Mission of God

Discuss the story in paragraph one. Use the following questions to expand the concept to today and your church:

What is your role in God's plan?

    As an individual?

    As a church?

What does the word "missionary" mean to you?

In what ways do you know you are God's people?

Read 1 Peter 2:9-10 and discuss.

What does it mean for a church to be inclusive?

In what ways does your church model inclusiveness
- to people of different color and race?
- to people of different abilities and needs?
- to women as well as men?
- to children and youth as well as adults?
- to people who have physical or mental disabilities?

In light of what Jesus did and said—

What would Jesus have the church do today?

What would Jesus have each of us do today?

In what ways does our church mission to people in body? mind? soul?

What do we know about the needs in the world in which we live?

Name three global needs.

Name three national needs.

Name three needs in your state or county.

Name three needs in your church neighborhood.

In what ways are you as the people of God responding to these needs?

What are some values that tend to get in the way of mission?

Name some missioners in your church. What are they doing?

Invite a missionary to come to class and talk about his or her mission—why he or she does it, his or her plans/goals, the need to which he or she responds.

Explore the ways you all do mission each day.

Discuss qualities/characteristics of a missioner.

What is the role of discipline in the life of your church?

Name some disciplines people act out in their own lives.

Discuss the benefits and struggles of maintaining discipline.

List three of your church's current goals related to mission.

List three new goals you'd like to implement related to mission.

Invite someone to relate some of your church's history in regards to mission.

Explore the beliefs your church membership holds about mission.

How do those beliefs empower you to effective action?

How do those beliefs block or hinder effective action?

Chapter 2 Education for Mission

Does your church have a plan for mission education?

Who do you look to in your church for mission education?

Consider each age group in your congregation.

What are the needs/resources of each group?

How is education for mission carried out at each age level?

How do new members learn about mission in your church?

Consider the steps in how people learn on pages_____.

Discuss ways that biblical persons have responded to the call to mission.

Invite members of your group to share their experiences being missioners.

Discuss your stories in relation to God's promise.

Discuss ways that people would like to change or repeat their mission experiences.

Look at ways individuals and/or the class want/s to do mission now and in the near future.

Talk about the educational process and its effectiveness.

Another way to study this session would be to have members discuss their involvement in mission now as individuals and as a congregation. How did education affect your mission perspective and activities? List what you'd like people at each age level to know about mission.

Examine your current educational program for missions.

In what ways is your present program meeting your needs and goals?

In what ways is your present program not meeting your
needs and goals?

If applicable, what must be done to reach what you'd
like to have happen in your mission program?

Chapter 3 Mission and Vocation/Avocation

Read the vignette and discuss.

Ask each person in the group to write down his or her
vocation.

Ask each to list his or her avocations.

On the chalkboard or newsprint list all the vocations of
the group.

In a separate space list all the avocations.

Discuss observations from the lists.

Talk about ways you are being missioners in your vocations and avocations.

Consider and discuss the concept of the call and whether
or not members feel called to both vocations and avocations.

Think about and discuss the questions on page 00.

Who am I?

What do I believe? about people about creation? about
money? about the good life? about being a Christian?

What am I about?

Ask participants to respond to the checklist in Appendix
2, "Lexicon for a New Church." Discuss the responses in
relation to the concept of missioners and vocation/avoca-
tion as described in chapter 3. (For those who may not
know, in #10, *laos* is the Greek word for people of God.)

Individually and as a group, list each member's gifts.

Consider ways this group can resource each other
about opportunities.

Discuss the following:

How does our church help people of all ages recognize
their gifts and opportunities?

In what ways does our church help people of all ages
develop their gifts? in the church community? eco-

nomically? globally?

In what ways does our church help people regain a sense of wonder? regain daydreams and adventures? nurture its members? learn to deal with power and bureaucracy? develop spiritual skills? express inclusiveness?

If we looked at our church as one body, what would we name as its vocation? as its avocation?

Chapter 4 Mission and Evangelism

Invite members of your group to define evangelism. How did they define it as they grew up in the church? How do they define it now?

Ask those who are familiar with the mission work of your denomination to tell about evangelism. How has it changed over the years? In what way? In what ways is it the same?

Discuss the five lessons about evangelism and mission.

1. Ultimately, evangelism and mission are God's work—in full partnership with God's people. Discuss the two poles of thinking:

• Ultimately God is in control, so it doesn't matter what men and women do.

• Humanity has free will—it is in our power and is our responsibility to evangelize the world.

How does the church function in each case? What evidence can you see in our society and in your lives for each way of thinking? What is the balance between the two statements? Where does your church fit in this perspective?

2. There is no authentic evangelism apart from mission, nor authentic mission apart from evangelism. Discuss this statement in light of your church's mission focus. Is the church evangelizing when it sponsors a soup kitchen or opens its doors to victims of oppression and disaster?

Can the church announce God's love and grace without showing them in deed?

3. Persons have the right to say no to us and reject our efforts of word and work—evangelism and mission. What does it mean to be a "faithful" partner with God? Is there ever a time when we accept a person's or a country's no and leave them alone? How do we as Christians decide when to persist and when to abandon our efforts?

4. Evangelism and mission are modeled in leadership. In what ways do we model evangelism and mission as individuals? as a church? In what ways could we model them locally? nationally? globally?

5. Evangelism and mission are a two-way street. In what areas does our church need to be missioned to? to be evangelized to? What skills do we need to learn to be more effective as a teaching church that takes mission seriously?

Chapter 5 The Teaching Church and Corporate Mission

Discuss your church's involvement in shared ministry.

- Does your pastor interact with other denominational people? In what instances? Do your laypeople?
- In what ways does your church mission? Why did you choose to work together through ecumenical efforts?
- Are there any ecumenical efforts in your community that you have chosen not to join? Why not?
- What mission plans do you have that might better be carried out through a cooperative and joint effort?
- What is the awareness and involvement of your church in political efforts?
- Do you support a social action committee or team?
- How do you gain information about social, community, and political proposals and actions?

This session might be enhanced by inviting a resource person—a politician/community action leader or a layperson or clergyperson from another denomination. Invite the resource person to tell about his or her work, and explore ways your church might cooperate in a mission venture.

Chapter 6 The Teaching Church and Planning

Discuss the various methods of planning in your church. Pick one or two plans and evaluate them using the following guidelines:

How are goals established? Who decides?

Do all people involved understand the goals and agree that they want to carry them out?

Were a number of options explored as to how to accomplish the goals?

Is the action plan clear?

Do all people involved know what they are expected to do?

Do all people involved know who is doing what?

Have you identified resources and materials needed?

Have you allocated money to this goal accomplishment?

Is there a time frame or a deadline?

How will you know you have accomplished your goal?

Do you take time to recognize and celebrate accomplishment?

As a group:

Consider a future goal and be intentional about formulating the plans.

Invite a planning expert to help your church do effective planning.

Resources for Further Study

Chartier, Jan, *Developing Leadership in the Teaching Church*. Valley Forge: Judson Press, 1985.

Hanson, Grant W., *Foundation for the Teaching Church*. Valley Forge: Judson Press, 1986.

Jones, Stephen D., *Transforming Discipleship in the Inclusive Church*. Valley Forge: Judson Press, 1984.

Lindgren, Alvin J., and Shawchuck, Norman, *Let My People Go: Empowering Laity for Ministry*. Nashville: Abingdon Press, 1980.

Peck, George, and Hoffman, John S., ed., *The Laity in Ministry*. Valley Forge: Judson Press, 1984.

Sine, Tom, *Taking Discipleship Seriously*. Valley Forge: Judson Press, 1985.

Wilson, Marlene, *How to Mobilize Church Volunteers*. Minneapolis: Augsburg Publishing House, 1983.

Appendix 2

Lexicon for a New Church or Word Power for the People of God ● Nelvin Vos

On January 1, 1988, according to plan, a new church of some five million members will be formed in the U.S. The new body, consisting of the American Lutheran Church, the Lutheran Church in America, and the Association of Evangelical Lutheran Churches, has been working on a plan for merger for the last several years.

The opening sentence of the Statement of Purpose of the new church is a ringing manifesto: "The Church is a people created by God in Christ, empowered by the Holy Spirit, called and sent to bear witness to God's creative, redeeming, and sanctifying activity in the world." The Church . . . in the world: these words open and close this key sentence. Such a church is clearly stating that it takes the ministry of the whole people of God seriously.

For the past ten years, I have been listening to and talking with members of these churches at retreats, conferences, and workshops on the ministry of the laity. I have been keeping my eyes and ears open to how key words are used by laity, pastors, and church leaders. For language, as we are all aware, is a mirror of our attitudes and thought patterns.

I therefore submit, on the basis of my listening and observation, a lexicon as my modest contribution to this new church and to all churches who are attempting to nurture the ministry of all God's people. I submit it with seriousness and, now and then, a touch of whimsy. Two notes for readers: (1) the multiple choices mean that you may select all of the answers, one of the answers, or none, and (2) occasionally, as any lexicon will do, an entry will include a citation.

So here goes:

1. **active member**
   - ☐ A.   a person involved in church doings
   - ☐ B.   a person involved in ministry in the church and in the world

2. **anti-lay**
   - ☐ A.   a term not yet coined
   - ☐ B.   in contrast to anti-clerical which some clergy say they sense fairly frequently

3. **baptism**
   - ☐ A.   a nice time for the family
   - ☐ B.   insurance policy for the hereafter
   - ☐ C.   the beginning of our ministry with the promise of forgiveness in Jesus Christ

4. **call**
   - ☐ A.   what only clergy receive
   - ☐ B.   a response to God's presence in where each of us is

5. **church**
   - ☐ A.   a place to come to and to go from
   - ☐ B.   a club to belong to
   - ☐ C.   who we are wherever we go

6. **confirmation**
   - ☐ A.   a graduation from Sunday church school
   - ☐ B.   a stepping-stone in a life of ministry

7. **congregation**

☐ A. a group of persons surrounding a clergyperson

☐ B. a community ministering both to one another and to those around them in the world

8. **full-time,** as in full-time Christian service or full-time ministry

☐ A. pastors

☐ B. missionaries

☐ C. all the people of God

Citation:

> "Have a look at your vocation. Ask yourself a question: 'Will this make a difference to the world when I'm through?' A veterinarian decided his thriving practice wouldn't. ('I was spending as much time with the owners as with the animals.') He entered the full-time ministry." (The *Lutheran,* January 7, 1981)

Also, occasionally used by second-career seminarians: "I decided to enter *the* ministry because in my previous occupation I did not feel I was in full-time Christian service."

Citation: Headline in seminary newsletter: Judge Chooses Ministry.
Excerpt from news item:

> "He had always felt drawn to the ministry but couldn't picture himself as a minister. 'Many of the priests and ministers I knew acted like they had a belly ache. I thought I was too worldly.' He saw much pathos in his almost 11 years as an assistant district attorney and district court judge. 'There were some very moving experiences. I felt people were coming to me with problems that were really spiritual problems and I didn't feel equipped to help them.'"

9. **gifts**

☐ A. what we share with one another at the time of birthdays

☐ B. the characteristics, skills, and talents God has bestowed on each of us

10. *laos*

☐ A. a country in southeast Asia

☐ B. the new people of God

Citation: "But you are . . . God's own people . . ." (1 Peter 2:9).

11. **lay**

☐ A. amateur, uninformed, as in "I'm only a lay person!"

☐ B. the non-ordained

12. **lay ministry**

☐ A. making lay people look and act like clergy

☐ B. what certain people do ("Lay ministry! I'm not into that!")

13. **liturgy**

☐ A. the work of the people

☐ B. what clergy decide is relevant for the people in the pews

☐ C. connecting our worship with our daily lives in the world

14. **member**

☐ A. one who pays dues and belongs to a group, as in PTA member

☐ B. one who is a living part of the body of Christ

15. minister (noun)

☐ A. pastors only

☐ B. all who respond to the calling to be servants of Jesus Christ

Citations:

"They shouldn't be called that; after all, I'm the only minister in this place."

"I don't want to be called that; it's expecting too much of me."

"Will all the ministers please stand up?" asked a pastor at a Reformation Day service. No one else stood up.

16. minister (verb)

☐ A. What only church leaders do ("After all, they get paid to do that.")

☐ B. to serve, to care, to love, to be available, to be a Christ to another

17. ministry

☐ A. what you and I do on our own steam

☐ B. a matter of status

☐ C. God working in and through us as we respond to the presence of Christ and the Holy Spirit in our lives

18. ministry of the laity

"In a 1½-year study of 29 urban congregations, mostly Lutheran, members (unordained and ordained) of the congregations developed the definitions below of the ministry of the laity, that is, of the people of God. The figures indicate the percentage of people who felt that particular arena was part of the ministry of the laity. From CSCM Yearbook cited by the Alban Institute.

☐ A. Doing things at church----70%

☐ B. Getting others to do things at church----15%

☐ C. Doing your best in vocation and job as a Christian----10%

☐ D. Relating and responding to others in their human need and potential----3%

☐ E. Recognizing, sharing and celebrating what Jesus Christ means in all of life----2%

19. ministry to the laity

☐ A. a set of skills certain professional people have who perform them on non-professionals

☐ B. listless passivity resulting in "the taming of the pew"

20. mutual ministry

☐ A. supporting the pastor

☐ B. supportive partnership with one another in order to be in ministry in the church and in the world

21. stewardship

☐ A. the total responsibility of all that God has entrusted to us

☐ B. time, money, and talents to be used for God

☐ C. money given to the church

22. **success**

☐ A. what Christians in ministry often expect, especially of themselves

☐ B. as opposed to faithfulness in which God both encourages and forgives us

23. **vacant congregation**

☐ A. the church which is without a pastor

☐ B. a time to assess what has been and could be done in ministry in that part of the body of Christ

24. **vocation**

☐ A. an occupation

☐ B. the expression of ministry of Christ in all our relationships

☐ C. the calling to a life in Christ and to faithful service in the world

Citation: In a 1977 survey, two thousand clergy and lay persons in the Lutheran Church in America were asked: When you think of the word *vocation,* which of the following comes to your mind most readily?

	Clergy	Lay Persons
God wants us to live a responsible Christian life in whatever we do	68%	11%
God calls one to enter some specific occupation as doctor or teacher	13%	14%
An occupation	14%	65%
Ordained ministry		1%
Full-time Christian work		1%
The word is unfamiliar		3%

25. volunteer

☐ A. a person willing to help another

☐ B. "It's entirely up to me whether I want to do this or not."

☐ C. the silence that follows: "Will anyone in the group. . . .?"

☐ D. as opposed to being drafted and enlisted in the service of Christ

26. world

☐ A. what Christians live in but not of

☐ B. "you are in the light of the _____"

☐ C. the arena of our ministry to one another

☐ D. God so loved the _____

Citation:

"I guess what I've learned this weekend is that I always thought I was in the world to go to church; now I see what I should have seen a long time ago, that I'm in the church in order to go into the world." Yellow Lines truck driver at end of retreat.

Nelvin Vos is Professor of English at Muhlenberg College, Allentown, Pennsylvania, U.S.A. and an active leader in the *Laos in Ministry* movement in the Lutheran Church of America.